HOPE IS NOT A STRATEGY

CHRISTIAN UNDERWOOD
JÜRGEN WEIGAND

HOPE IS NOT A STRATEGY

StrategyFrame®:
The smart way to make strategy work

Campus Verlag
Frankfurt/New York

Bibliographic Information published by the Deutsche Nationalbibliothek. The Deutsche Nationalbibliothek lists this publication in the Deutsche Nationalbibliografie; detailed bibliographic data are
available on the Internet at http://dnb.d-nb.de.

ISBN 978-3-593-51709-4 Print
ISBN 978-3-593-45387-3 E-Book (PDF)

Cover design, interior design, graphic design and typesetting:
ZIMMERMANN – Büro für visuelle Kommunikation

Printing office and bookbinder: Beltz Grafische Betriebe GmbH, Bad Langensalza
Beltz Grafische Betriebe is a climate-neutral company (ID 15985-2104-1001)

Printed in Germany
www.campus.de
www.press.uchicago.edu

For Zoe and Brit

For Nicole, Sebastian and Sammy

CONTENTS

STRATEGY DEVELOPMENT

STRATEGY EXECUTION

PREFACE

We began in 2020 with our podcast "HOFFNUNG IST KEINE STRATEGIE" [HOPE IS NOT A STRATEGY]. During the many years we worked in management consultancy and management training, we discovered time and again that for many decision-makers, managers or employees, the word strategy denotes something mysterious, abstract, academic, or maybe even esoteric. And this is a fact despite an overwhelming range of university and non-academic management education and training courses, consultancy services of all flavors, smart specialist and reference books and countless "online tools". We wanted to demystify the "strategy" myth and find out why strategy work is often neglected, implemented poorly, or, if it is to be provided by third parties, regarded as unaffordable.

In short, when we considered the many podcast discussions with amazing strategists from all enterprise classes, from SMEs to big corporations, the countless comments and queries from our now more than five thousand subscribers, as well as our own experience, one thing became clear to us very quickly: The last word has not yet been said about strategy.

However, we do not have to reinvent the strategy wheel. On the contrary: We are convinced that all the theories, concepts and tools that are required for good strategy work already exist. To paraphrase Isaac Newton's famous quotation: We can see further by standing on the shoulders of strategy giants. But how do we best check what is already available for usefulness, merge it, and use it?

This "workbook" does that for you. You no longer need to shy away from the big word: "strategy". We will dispel your reservations and provide you with a tried and tested manual on how you can make your company flourish with a cleverly designed strategy process – from strategy development to implementation and beyond.

Learning is most effective when you can immediately try out or implement what you learned. The strategy process is an excellent place for organizational learning. Our workbook uses the "workflow learning" approach to provide you with precise contextual and timely support for your strategy work when you need it. In a continuous and transparent workflow, you develop the strategy with your team and implement it step by step. But that is not all: Our shared journey also leads into digital space: You will find all the materials in this book to download at www.campus.de/hopeisnotastrategy. If you wish to create your strategy in the digital domain, we offer you a brand-new strategy software and platform that can provide everything that your strategy process still lacks, or make it smarter and more effective, on www.Strategy-Frame.com.

Together, we will make strategy your new routine. From tomorrow, you will no longer train your operational muscle alone but your strategic muscle too at last. As we know, it is easier to stand on two legs.

We hope this book gives you strategic inspiration for your daily operations!

Sincerely,
Christian Underwood & Jürgen Weigand
Düsseldorf & Vallendar, Germany, November 2022

All the materials of this book for download
campus.de/hopeisnotastrategy

Everything you need for the digital strategy process
strategy-frame.com

The podcast to the book
hope-is-not-a-strategy.com

The download materials and discounted access to the digital StrategyFrame® are protected by a password, which you will find in this book. It is three words from this book. The first one you will find on page 50, line 9, word number 3. Word number 2 we have hidden on page 120, line 9 in the 2nd place. Lastly, pick out the 1st word on line 28 on page 254. Type this combination without spaces into the input mask to access the download materials or the digital StrategyFrame®.

STRATEGY

SUPREME DISCIPLINE OR WASTE OF TIME?

"Strategy is a big word. Sometimes oversized. When it is used in a meeting, everyone solidifies into a pillar of salt, and everyone hopes for the Messiah who will show the way. But we must realize that strategy is often just a weak person's failsafe. Strategy is important (…) for the person who doesn't make it by sheer toil and effort."
Holger Jung and Jean Remy von Matt, *Momentum* (2002)

Many managers and business leaders glorify strategy development as the supreme discipline of company management. Others, like the German advertising gurus quoted above, regard strategy development as a waste of time. This is the polarized reality after a discussion about the whole purpose of strategy that has continued for more than 100 years. And the general understanding of strategy is somewhere in between these two poles.

Everyone knows the term, and everyone associates it with something different, depending on the context. Strategy is ambivalent and fraught with reservations. On the one hand, we understand that strategy is about intentional and focused action with rational logic behind it. On the other hand, strategy has a certain dazzling quality but also something mysterious, disreputable, and dangerous, because it is frequently associated subliminally with images of generating a relative superiority with which to deceive, trick, and take advantage of others, and is therefore correlated with morally questionable behavior. And these prejudices have an impact! In practice, this ambivalence for one thing causes strategy as a topic to be misunderstood, consciously or subconsciously, either out of self-interest or self-preservation. Because we handle anything we cannot fully understand, describe, or grasp with skepticism, rejection or even with fear.

What is strategy?

So, let us start at the beginning. What is strategy? To us, the simplest answer is: Strategy is the path we want to take in order to get from our today to our desired future. The basis of strategy is a clear picture of what our future should look like and of what we need to get there. For Jack Welch, the former chairman and CEO of General Electric, strategy was very straightforward: "You pick a general direction and implement like hell." But if we do not know where we want to get to, we will end up who knows where. Then, sheer toil and effort, as our advertising gurus claimed, will not be enough.

When company managers think about their "strategy", they are usually thinking about nothing less than the general direction of the company as well as the key issues and measures to ensure its future viability. But in fact, they wrestle with budgets and crunch numbers in forecast and planning sessions. Even the annually recurring "retreats" customary in many large companies, where management teams temporarily lock themselves away in monasteries, extravagant conference venues, and other attractive locations "offsite" for closed strategy meetings, seldom contribute to the systematic formulation of strategic thought and action within a company or to the continuous development of corporate strategy.

That doesn't matter, anti-strategists may argue at this point. What should a person strategically plan in a complex world full of disruptions and unlawful developments, where only one thing is certain: that the future is uncertain. What was it that Albert Einstein said? "I never think about the future. It comes soon enough." That is why company managers who are stuck in the here and now dare to perform a balancing act: They only respond to changes when they occur – with agility, flexibility, and resilience. Lovely buzzwords! In an overestimation of their own capability, or even with a sense of genius, these high-wire walkers prefer to obey the well-known "law" of the Rhineland (geographic and cultural area in Germany): "Et hätt noch emmer jot jejangen." Meaning: It always turned out ok before. But hoping for the best as a guiding principle has seldom turned out ok – neither in a big corporation nor in an SME that was once a "hidden champion". Nothing works without a strategy – or if it does, then only by chance.

Even if there is a strategy, company management is by no means home and dry yet. Do the employees know and understand the strategy? Do they believe in its feasibility and success? A survey conducted by consulting firm strategy& in 2019 among 6,000 management executives reached a dramatic conclusion: 75 percent of respondents stated that they did not believe in the success of their own company's strategy, 19 percent responded that there was no guiding strategy in their company at all, while 33 percent believed that the problem was the difficult and protracted implementation, since market conditions change rapidly and constantly. Thus, according to other studies carried out by Sull et al. (2015) as well as by Collis (2021), around two-thirds of all corporate strategies fail at the implementation stage.

Results like these are grist to the mill for those who view strategy as a waste of time. For this reason, strategists must tackle the question of why strategy should be more than "art for art's sake" and why it evidently so seldom works.

From our experience of strategy processes in different company situations, there are three factors that must converge to ensure the successful formulation and implementation of a corporate strategy:

Three success factors

1. There has to be a clear definition and a common understanding about what strategy precisely means and entails.
2. A systematic and analytical approach is essential for the development of a strategy in order not to end up in randomness and who knows where.
3. Implementing a strategy requires a disciplined, structured process where coordination and communication are essential.

From our experience of what works in practice and what does not, we have developed a simple thought and action framework, the StrategyFrame®, which helps strategists fulfil these three factors.

A SMALL SHEET OF PAPER AND ITS CONSEQUENCES

When we ask management executives at the start of a training seminar or consultancy brief to formulate their company's strategy briefly and concisely on the small sheet of notepaper in front of them, a strange silence generally ensues. They obviously had not expected this kick-off. They think in silence. "You have 3 minutes." Time pressure. They finish. "Why don't you read out what you have written." What follows are descriptions of "strategies" like: "Our strategy has four value levers: innovative product solutions, optimized operational performance, customer orientation, and sustainability," "We achieve profitable growth through strategic capital allocation," or "We are volume leaders in … and offer our customers value for money." All clear so far?

Nothing is clear. In the critical discussion that follows, these descriptive attempts quickly reveal themselves to be merely series of empty words. What exactly do "innovative", "optimized", or "strategic" mean? We provoke them a little further: "Profitable growth" is a target, not a strategy! And on top of that, it is not specific. "What" precisely is supposed to grow, "why", and "how far"? Is the sky the limit? When will growth become profitable?

The management executives' blood pressure rises. They switch to defensive and justification mode. "Our customer feedback is excellent, so we must be doing something right." That's true. But what about the customers who do not buy from you? "We are market leaders; you must be able to gather that from our 22 percent market share. That is an objective measurement." Agreed, but as Bruce Henderson (1989), founder of consultancy firm BCG, commented:

"Market share is a meaningless number unless a company defines the market in terms of the boundaries separating it from its rivals."

What Henderson is saying is that quantifying a market position does not answer either the "why" or the "how". Why do you think, or why can you measurably prove, that you are a market leader? Because you are a big fish in a small pond? What differentiates the big fish from the small rivals? How did it achieve this market position? And furthermore: If we just make the definition of our pond narrow enough, our market share will rise to 100 percent. Here is one example: Coca-Cola's market share in the global market for carbonated soft drinks was 24.3 percent in 2021. In the US market, it was 46.3 percent (Statista, 2023). However, Coca-Cola's market share in both the global and US market for carbonated soft drinks of the Coca-Cola brand is 100 percent.

We stick to our Socratic approach and subsequently ask: How profitable is it to be a big fish? Answer: "Of course we are profitable." That's awesome, congratulations! But couldn't you do even better if the pond was bigger, or even if it was a different pond? Now the discussion becomes heated and reaches its climax. "We're not strategically positioned for a bigger pond." Ok, so you don't have an expansion plan. "And anyway, what do you mean by a different pond? Should we start selling insurance tomorrow, or what?"

We thank the management executives we had blindsided with our strategy question for their enlightening contributions to the discussion and reassure them: they are in good company. As Markides (2022) points out in the *Harvard Business Review,* many company strategists confuse targets and strategy. Effective strategy formulas require a common understanding of strategy. In practice, however, it is rare that much time is spent on clarifying terminology and the assumptions, ideas, and interpretations underlying it in order to reach a workable formulation of strategy which then really does fit on a sheet of notepaper and is comprehensible. In strategy processes, a great deal of time, countless discussion sessions, and hundreds of PowerPoint slides are frequently spent on activities that can be described as "planning". But strategy is a plan, not planning.

We still have one last question for the management executives, and we ask them for an honest and unemotional answer: "If your company no longer existed tomorrow, would anyone miss it?" Our honest answer: The majority of respondents come to the conclusion that their companies' customers would not miss them very long and would find a replacement for them relatively quickly. But if you can be replaced quickly, what distinguishes you from your rivals? Is "we too" an adequate reason for being? What is your plan for being relevant in the future? Tough questions to which the strategists must find answers. As management theorist and strategy pioneer Henry Mintzberg (1994, p. 333) emphasizes, strategy is not the consequence of planning but rather its starting point. And thus necessary.

THE NECESSARY INSIGHT

"Strategy" as a term, concept and usage originated in the military field. The word "strategy" is derived from the Ancient Greek – "strategia": to lead an army ("stratos"). The "strategos" is the leader of the army. He/she provides direction – where the troops should be deployed – and dictates the focus – which battles should be fought where and when. How the troops operate, what measures they take in order to win, depends on the one hand on the terrain in which they are moving, and on the other hand on their reservoir of tactical capabilities and how they use this reservoir to implement the strategy they are pursuing.

In the field of business, the "company" is the army. The "leaders" are usually either the company founders, their heirs, or appointed management executives. The main task of company management is to organize the company, define the core goals, make the necessary resources available, and lead the organization so that it fulfils its tasks profitably. Business historian Alfred D. Chandler (1962) provided the classical definition of strategy in *Strategy and Structure*, his groundbreaking study of the success factors in large corporations: "… strategy is the determination of the basic long-term goals and objectives of an enterprise, and the adoption of courses of action and the allocation of resources necessary for carrying out these goals."

The classical definition of strategy

We live in a world of limited resources. Hence, companies are compelled to operate efficiently. That means making optimum use of available resources and avoiding waste. They must develop strategies that can be implemented with these resources. If the resources are available, efficient operations are a zero-sum game: Whatever we use the resources for will reduce their availability for alternative allocations. If we want to invest more money in one company area, we have to save the "more" in other areas. Thus, distributing company resources is liable to goal conflicts and requires decisions that weigh up the benefits and costs of each allocation ("trade-offs"). It is the task of company executives to make these decisions. Therefore, the finite nature of resources is the first fundamental reason why strategy is needed.

Limited resources

The second fundamental reason is competition. Companies never operate in a vacuum. They compete with others. Even if they have an outstanding market position, they are vulnerable. Let us take Intel as an example. For a long time, the US company was the global market leader in microprocessors for computers, with a market share of more than 80 percent, followed only by AMD with a market share below 20 percent. Since 2016, Intel's market share has shrunk continually to just under 60 percent, while AMD has doubled its market share. What happened? Intel's competitive advantage stemmed from superior product technology, excellence in production, and a strong brand ("Intel inside"). Spoiled by their success, the company had underestimated the upheavals taking place in technology and in the use of microprocessors. The smartphone revolution passed them by. After making massive investments in supermodern production technology and capacity in this industry segment, Taiwanese company TSCM established itself as market leader with a market share of more than 50 percent, leaving both Samsung and Intel far behind. As well as producing microprocessors for smartphones and the automobile industry, TSCM is also a highly efficient contract manufacturer for AMD's innovative microprocessors. With lower costs, better manufacturing and higher product quality thanks to its cooperation with TSCM, AMD significantly improved its market share to the detriment of Intel.

The competition between Intel and AMD appears to be a zero-sum game, because AMD has gained about 20 percentage points in market share, while Intel lost this size share. But competition does not necessarily deliver an "I-win-what-you-lose" result. Instead, competition is often a non-zero-sum game. For example, when competition leads to better products and increased demand, all competitors can profit. A "win-win" situation emerges. Conversely, a price war leads to a "win" for customers but to a "lose-lose" for the competing companies.

Now the challenge for your company lies in mastering the two opposing "games" – the internal allocation game and the external competition game – simultaneously, and additionally under time pressure, in environments that are difficult to read because of systemic complexity and volatile dynamics. It requires strategic thought and action, meaning acting instead of reacting. But how should we act? By first asking and answering the following relevant questions.

THE QUESTIONS YOU SHOULD ASK AND ANSWER

In a nutshell, strategy is the mandatory response to the reality of limited resources and of competition in constantly changing environments. It is a risky bet on an uncertain future. To ensure they do not become victims of this future, strategists should attempt to shape the future proactively. To do this, five fundamental questions should be answered:

#1: WHAT DO WE WANT TO ACHIEVE?

Business enterprises are profit oriented. Their core financial goal is profitability: The return on the capital invested should exceed the cost of using equity and debt capital.

#2: WHO DEFINES WHAT THE COMPANY SHOULD STRIVE FOR, WHO MAKES THE GOAL-RELATED DECISIONS, AND WHO SHOULD EXECUTE THEM?

It is the responsibility of company management to set the course for the company, define the goals, set priorities, delineate the master plan for the envisaged activities, make the necessary resources available, create adequate structures and processes for implementing the strategy, and monitor the execution of the strategy.

#3: WHY AND FOR WHOM DO WE WANT TO ACHIEVE THESE SPECIFIC GOALS?

Strategy requires clarity about the purpose of the company and a perspective for the future. Company management must map out the long-term intention for the company in a meaningful "narrative", and also paint a convincing picture of what the future could look like if the envisaged strategy is realized, and what this means for the various stakeholders in the company.

#4: WHERE AND WHEN DO WE WANT TO DEPLOY OUR RESOURCES AND COMPETENCIES?

A corporate strategy specifies where, when and within what scope the company will operate. Since the available resources are limited, the internal zero-sum game we previously described occurs here. Potential courses of action must be considered as to whether they are substitutive in their consumption of resources, and thus lead to allocation conflicts, or whether they potentially complement each other and create viable synergies.

These allocation questions must be decided by the highest level of management with the aim of finding the company's optimum adaptation to its field of activity. Creating the right strategic "fit" is an ongoing task. Because the strategic environment is constantly changing, the strategy's sustained applicability must be constantly reviewed.

#5: HOW SHOULD RESOURCES AND COMPETENCIES BE DEPLOYED?

A key element of corporate strategy consists of determining how a company should position itself in its various business fields and focus markets and which instruments it should use to acquire profitable customers and keep the competition at bay. A competitive strategy coherently stipulates and integrates the required functional strategy elements, such as marketing, distribution, human resources, and research & development.

The answers to these five core questions will establish how the company wants to optimally use available resources, capital and employees, in competition to realize profits. Since there is seldom a lack of competition, strategy development is predominantly a question of how the company can rise above the competition in the various areas of activity.

THE TRUTH LIES ON THE FIELD

What do you do when the good old competition or new opponents cunningly and aggressively attempt to snatch away some of your market share, or even try to drive you out of the market? When the adversaries torpedo your value proposition to your customers with similar offers and predatory pricing? When the rules of the game in your sector abruptly change and yesterday's success no longer counts for anything today? Keep a cool head, take a step back and analyze the current situation carefully. Who are the relevant opponents, the current and potential future ones? What distinguishes them? What are their weaknesses? Who are their customers? What do they want? How can you acquire and retain profitable customers?

Strategy is your plan for how your company should be different so that it can hold sway over the competition, and for which resources and skills you need to do this. In the words of master strategist Michael Porter (1996):

"Competitive strategy is about being different. It means deliberately choosing a different set of activities to deliver a unique mix of value."

German football coach and player Otto Rehagel famously said: "The truth lies on the field" – meaning that it is measured by the number of goals scored. We need players who can score goals. At the same time, we need players who prevent the opponent from scoring goals. And we have to let everyone on the team play in such a way that they score more goals than the opponent. "Let[ting] them play in such a way" is the game plan or strategy: defensive or offensive play, aggressive interception and fast switching, high ball possession or counterattack, etc. The tactical measures are the rehearsed or improvised moves that are chosen by the players at short notice during their interaction with the opponent.

For companies, the truth is revealed in the market and is measured by the profitability of what has been achieved. You have to have the capability to deploy your limited resources in such a way that you rise above your rivals and are chosen by customers. To achieve this otherness, the strategist's first task is to decide what not to do (Porter, 1996, p. 70). And that is no easy decision.

MAKE BETTER DECISIONS

Every day, we make around 20,000 decisions. But we only adopt a very small proportion of these decisions consciously, reflecting on them and weighing up costs against benefits. Unlike in academic models of economic decision making, our rationality is bounded. We decide under time pressure, with incomplete information, and impaired by systematic errors of judgment.

Human decision-making processes follow the economic principle which implies reaching a decision with the smallest possible effort (time, processing capacity, etc.). We therefore use simplifying heuristics, even for very complex and momentous decisions, to compensate for our limited rationality. In this process, we intuitively tend to have recourse to our prior experience – and this is where it gets dangerous.

On the one hand, in an era of disruptive and interdependent social and economic transformation processes (digitalization, sustainability, etc.), prior experience ceases to be a competitive advantage. When several variables in a conditional equation simultaneously change radically, the algebra of Management 101 is no longer sufficient to estimate the consequences of the results.

On the other hand, subconscious cognitive distortions, such as anchoring effects, confirmation bias, or selective information processing, foster errors of judgement. If, for example, a decision-making situation is similar to an earlier one, the experience gained and the results achieved in the earlier situation can become an anchor in the new situation if the actual comparability of the situations is not adequately reviewed. Having an awareness of cognitive distortions should be a top priority for strategists, especially when making complex strategic decisions.

Strategic decisions differ fundamentally from tactical or operational measures. Willie Pietersen, Professor of the Practice of Management at Columbia Business School, New York, points out the difference in his seminars:

"We have to lay the railroad tracks first before we can make the trains run on time."

Strategy means committing to the future in a particular course of action – investing in tracks and laying them in a particular direction, to continue Pietersen's metaphor – and thus committing yourself. Self-commitment generates longer-term consequences. Therefore, strategic decisions cannot simply be reversed.

Once the railroad tracks have been laid, they cannot be re-laid in a new direction at short notice. In contrast, tactical measures, like the precise departure and arrival times of the trains, can be changed at short notice. The degree of self-commitment is minimal, and the modification costs are low.

Even if we do achieve an awareness of our limited rationality in making decisions, if we reduce information deficits and cognitive distortions, we are not home and dry yet. As Nobel Prize winner Daniel Kahnemann (2011) and his co-authors (2021) demonstrate, people in a decision-making situation can reach completely different conclusions and decisions from an identical starting point. Alongside cognitive distortions, Kahnemann et al. cite an additional determining factor: "noise". Wherever people make decisions, they are influenced by a considerable amount of interference that even in identical circumstances leads to different decisions depending on personality. These psychological factors also play a decisive role when defining and implementing a new strategy in a company. Then there are also the decision makers' personal values as well as the sociopsychological dynamics that arise, for example, at the annual closed strategy meeting because of the collaboration or conflict of different alpha personalities.

Stumbling blocks: cognitive distortions, interference, and personal values

Isn't all this just a question of process? Can we set up a decision-making process and make it so systematic that the risk of false conclusions is minimized?

TRUST THE PROCESS

We all have experience of group-based decision-making processes. Frequently, it was a negative experience. Company representatives report to us time and again about ineffective strategy processes that are demotivating and frustrating. Valuable time wasted in countless unstructured and thus fruitless discussion sessions, ego-driven image contests witnessed, and dozens of strategy updates observed. Only to realize at the end with a sinking feeling that the world didn't stop turning and that the entire effort will likely fail to have a significantly positive effect on the company or their own careers. Thus, it is no wonder that decision makers find it difficult to specify the significance and content of strategy and shape the required strategy process successfully.

The strategy process is a difficult project, much more difficult than formulating a strategy. When you have a difficult project, it can be beneficial to initially concentrate on – trust – what you can control – the process – and not the result. "Trust the process" is a familiar slogan used by fans of the Philadelphia 76ers in the US NBA that has now become popular in other fields too. It was coined while the team was going through a difficult phase and means: "Things might look bad now, but we have a plan to make things better."

That is the crux: We have a plan for how we want to improve. And that in itself is an asset in its own right for managing companies and the people in them. Instead of hoping for better days, a shared plan generates clarity and optimism to be able to actively shape and change our own future instead of becoming a pawn of universal market forces.

From our practical experience, we can identify four key problems in strategy processes:

1. The company strategy has only been vaguely formulated because there is no clarity or consensus at management level about the initial situation, target vision, and action areas. Particularly in larger companies with matrix structures, this invariably leads to contradictory strategies in the company areas and functional divisions. Too many parallel strategic projects emerge. Overview and communication, which should feed into company strategy, and which are interlinked, are lost.
2. There is no clear process architecture and only inadequate responsibilities for the envisaged implementation.
3. There is a lack of resources and routines for attending to strategy work alongside day-to-day operations.
4. The significance of strategy and its effectiveness is usually concealed by business operations and their short-term results in everyday business. Strategy is future-oriented and thus only delivers results with a time delay. If the results are bad, people quickly talk about the wrong strategy. In contrast, if they are good, they say the implementation was successful. This is how a lucky strike is quickly explained and subsequently attributed to strategic procedure. However, the extent to which strategic thought and action really contributed to the result that was achieved frequently remains an unknown entity. Furthermore, good operating results can be instant catapults for managers' careers. So why spend a long time thinking about strategy when the game is decided on the field – or rather in the market?

Are you discouraged now? Disappointed? Can we remove the obstacles, unsatisfactory realities, strategy legends, and human imperfections described above from the strategy process equation? How can strategy development be established in a company "end-to-end", from formulation right up to implementation? In these uncertain and volatile times, is there any sense in thinking about a strategy for a company at all anymore?

We believe: Yes, there is. Particularly in times of great uncertainty, it is not enough to hope that the right solution will fall from the sky. However, no new theories are required for the strategy debate either. Instead, what we need are approaches and instruments for strategy development and implementation that are also fit for purpose in a company's everyday business.

For this reason, over the past 15 years, we have developed a pragmatic instruction manual of strategic thought and action for strategists – our StrategyFrame® – and tested it thoroughly within companies in their specific business contexts. It provides a reference framework for an end-to-end strategy process. The Strategy-Frame® supports corporate leaders and their management teams in clarifying the initial situation, setting the strategic focus correctly, and defining the appropriate action areas, as well as prioritizing and tackling adaptation measures in the organization to achieve goals and maintain focus.

Our experience in business practice, in management training, and in the context of consulting have shown us this: Only those who gain clarity about their own situation, set their goals correctly, and know exactly who has to take action when, where, and how, can be in the right place at the right time with the right solution. The StrategyFrame® helps managers gain perspective, retain an overview, and develop foresight. A perfectly balanced strategy process can generate momentum in an organization because people want prospects, sound structures, transparent processes, and consistent actions – the overall picture has to be coherent. Not until they understand why the journey is heading where it is heading will they too come on board and pitch in energetically.

It's true: The game is decided on the field. But our strategy decides whether we are allowed to play, and how we can play. So, is strategy therefore the "supreme discipline" of company management? That is a matter of taste. But it is definitely not a waste of time but a necessity.

BEING AND STAYING RELEVANT

How relevant is your company on today's playing fields? If you are convinced of your own relevance, that's nice. But your opinion is irrelevant. What counts is the customer perspective. Therefore, you must ask the existential question you already know: If our company no longer existed tomorrow, would anyone miss it? If the customers' answer is "Yes, of course, they're not easy to replace!" then you have a reason for being, at least for a short time frame, and you are relevant. However, if the answer is, "No, not really, there are plenty of other providers we could switch to very easily!", then your company is a "we-too" case in the best-case scenario, and without substantial change will be pushed out by

If our company no longer existed tomorrow, would anyone miss it?

the competition sooner or later in the "perennial gale of creative destruction" (Schumpeter, 1942, pp. 82). It goes without saying that we hope for your sake that your customers would miss your company. But as John Maynard Keynes (1924, p. 80) formulated it in another context:

"In the long run we are all dead."

That means that even if you enjoy relevance and customer acceptance today, the question of your company's viability arises from the point of view of a longer time frame. Thus, strategy is the answer to the question of how your company can stay relevant.

"THE ESSENCE OF STRATEGY IS CHOOSING WHAT NOT TO DO."

Michael E. Porter, American economist and Professor,
Institute for Strategy and Competitiveness, Harvard Business School

STRATEGYFRAME®

AN INSTRUMENT FROM THE FIELD – FOR THE FIELD

Any company manager who sets a course for a new strategy will be inundated by clever concepts from academia, consultants, and self-proclaimed experts of all stripes. There is truly no lack of methods and instruments on the topic of strategy in relevant management books, trade magazines, and on the internet.

And the BCG Matrix, Porter's industry structure analysis (Five Forces), the Balanced Scorecard, PESTEL, CAGE, SWOT, Blue Ocean, or even the Business Canvas Model only form the tip of the iceberg. Why does the world of strategic company management need yet another strategy tool? Is the existing toolset not enough? Must we repeatedly sell the old wine in new wineskins?

These are the critical questions we asked ourselves too when we were developing our StrategyFrame® and ultimately when we were writing this book. Of course, the well-known tools have their justification in their respective areas of application, but unfortunately, they don't entirely meet the fundamental needs of today's strategists and their organizations. One deployment of these strategy tools, generally combined with elaborate Excel tables and extensive PowerPoint presentations, does not make a "strategy summer". Therefore, many strategy executives have a difficult time finding the right way to develop and implement a coherent and activating corporate strategy. After months of grueling strategy work alongside daily business operations, their enthusiasm and momentum have fallen by the wayside, and in the end, they are disappointed with the results.

From our work with strategy executives in both small and medium-sized companies as well as in large corporations, we know the questions that are on their minds:

What questions do you have?

- Which strategic thought and operational framework is the right one for us? Which elements does it comprise?
- How should we proceed methodically in developing and implementing our strategy?
- How can we execute the various elements of the strategy process efficiently and effectively?
- How do we create acceptance for the strategy we have developed?

These strategy practitioner's needs are what drove us to develop a simple, workable tool for the strategy process, from the formulation of a strategy right up to its implementation. The StrategyFrame® combines and visualizes the key elements of strategy work into one overall picture that gives context, content, process, and maybe even emotional orientation and clarity to all involved and to all stakeholders. Across its three core modules, the key fundamental questions – what must we know, what must we decide, and what must we do – are answered.

THE THREE CORE MODULES

1.

SITUATION ANALYSIS

Where do we stand today and what are our greatest challenges?

2.

TARGET VISION

Where do we want to go and what specific goals are we pursuing to get there?

3.

ACTION AREAS

Where do we need to take action and change things in our organization?

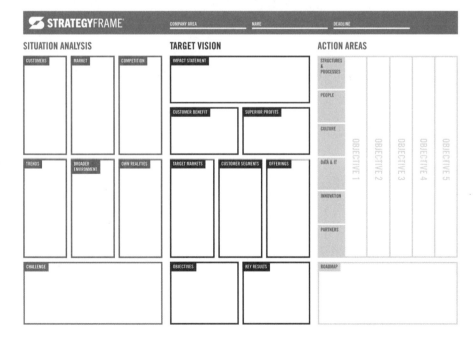

StrategyFrame®
overview

1. 2. 3.

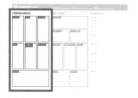

SITUATION ANALYSIS

It involves analyzing your company's situation in its current action areas, identifying potential new areas, and understanding the external environment. Answers must be found to the following questions: Where is your greatest potential in the "market"? Which markets are you addressing? What are the needs of the "customers" and how are they changing? Who are the "competition"? Which "trends" are changing your industry? What is happening in the "broader environment"? What do your "own realities" look like? And finally: Which "challenges" emerge for your company?

CUSTOMERS	MARKET	COMPETITION
TRENDS	BROADER ENVIRONMENT	OWN REALITIES

CHALLENGE

TARGET VISION

In the second core module, you will develop the "focus" of your corporate strategy on four target levels:

1. IMPACT

In your "impact statement" you will stipulate how your company aims to achieve a sustainable effect for business, the environment, and society.

2. CUSTOMER BENEFIT & SUPERIOR PROFITS

Your distinguishing "customer benefit" will clarify what your company intends to do better than or different from the competition, and thus generate "superior profits" so that you are a step ahead of the competition.

3. PLAYING FIELD

The key component of your focusing process is marking out the playing fields for your company. Which "target markets" do you want to be active in? Which "customer segments" do you want to address with which "offerings"? Which competitors are you entering the ring against?

4. PRIORITIES

When you define your "goals" and "key results", you define what is on the schedule in which order for your company. In this context, objectives and key results can be motivated by both quantitative and qualitative factors.

IMPACT STATEMENT		
CUSTOMER BENEFIT		SUPERIOR PROFITS
TARGET MARKETS	CUSTOMER SEGMENTS	OFFERINGS
OBJECTIVES		KEY RESULTS

ACTION AREAS

Once your target vision has been determined, the next task is realizing it. What actions do you and your team have to take within the company? Which "structures & processes" are necessary? How can "data & IT" be optimally utilized in the digital age? Which "people" with which skills does your company need? Which "culture" will unleash the power for "innovations"? Which strategic "partners" could help you to achieve your goals?

If your corporate strategy aims to impact various business units, geographies, and functional areas, you can specify the expected value contribution of the individual units at this stage.

To ensure that your strategy does not remain a mere declaration of intent, you should draw up a "timetable" for its implementation and for the transformation of your company. It will determine the "control" of timing and content, how the strategy will be "cascaded" through the individual business units, geographies, and functional areas, and which "dramaturgy" you would like to use for your actions in the various phases.

STRUCTURES & PROCESSES	OBJECTIVE 1	OBJECTIVE 2	OBJECTIVE 3	OBJECTIVE 4	OBJECTIVE 5
PEOPLE					
CULTURE					
DATA & IT					
INNOVATION					
PARTNERS					
ROADMAP					

A COMMON UNDERSTANDING

If you don't have a common vision of what is possible when you pursue a common strategy, it won't work. If you don't set out for the future from a common basis, your strategy work will involve a lot of friction losses and misunderstandings and therefore will not be very effective.

The modular StrategyFrame® provides clarity and an overview of all the elements that must be taken into account in strategy work. It helps identify potential gaps in strategic considerations, consolidates insights gained, makes the decisive points of the strategy directly visible to everyone in the company and does not hide them behind a gazillion PowerPoint slides. When you use the Strategy-Frame®, you will never lose sight of the overall context during the strategy process, but you will nonetheless get enough space to dive into the necessary details to gain true perspective.

Strategy at a glance

Thus, the StrategyFrame® acts as an organizational content platform for strategy development, whether for the initial or the regular strategy meeting, or for the annual review and adjustment of the strategy. At the same time, it can be used as a visual instrument for communicating with and involving employees or other stakeholders (investors, banks).

Central content platform

STRATEGYFRAME®

COMPANY AREA

SITUATION ANALYSIS

CUSTOMERS

MARKET

COMPETITION

TRENDS

BROADER ENVIRONMENT

OWN REALITIES

CHALLENGE

TARGET VISION

IMPACT STATEMENT

CUSTOMER BENEFIT

TARGET MARKETS

CUSTOMER SEGMENT

OBJECTIVES

NAME _____

DEADLINE _____

ACTION AREAS

		OBJECTIVE 1	OBJECTIVE 2	OBJECTIVE 3	OBJECTIVE 4	OBJECTIVE 5
STRUCTURES & PROCESSES						
PEOPLE						
CULTURE						
DATA & IT						
INNOVATION						
PARTNERS						

SUPERIOR PROFITS

FFERINGS

KEY RESULTS

ROADMAP

STRATEGY WORKFLOW

LEARNING AT THE MOMENT OF APPLICATION

"Learning is most effective in the doing. That is why the work process is an excellent place to learn. Performance support or workflow learning with a digital coach offer customized learning and support at the precise time when they are needed."
Oliver Kern, Performance Support Expert

Be honest: How many of the management books on your shelves have you actually read? How many of those were genuinely helpful to you in solving your business challenges? And which content and insights can you still remember one year later? In each case, the number is likely to be manageably low.

The 70:20:10 model sums it up as a simple formula: Developed in the 1980s by management researchers McCall, Lombardo, and Eichinger, the model demonstrates that we gain around 70 percent of our professional knowledge by daily "learning and doing on the job", while some 20 percent of our knowledge stems from colleagues and other people. Further training measures of all types (like traditional seminars or e-learning) contribute only 10 percent. The mere availability of attractive sources of knowledge is not enough for managers to actually use these purposefully. Time is a scarce and precious resource that no one willingly spends on dry knowledge transfer.

Instead, we have experienced that effective learning becomes manifest in its application and in the resulting experience gained. Comparable to how a flight simulator is used to train pilots, we use software-based simulations, for example, to train decision-making capacity and to test the consequences of strategic and operational decisions. Nothing sticks better in our minds than what we try out and experience ourselves.

Learning across the workflow

Today, we live in an era of information overload. More data is available than ever before. We are increasingly using artificial intelligence to channel the flow of data, to process data, and to interpret data. Despite the support of digital automation, strategy executives have to filter out the information that is relevant for decisions. What must be analyzed, thought through, discussed, and agreed, when and how, in the strategy process? It is easy to lose your overview in this process. Then information overload turns into brain overload, and overview turns into tunnel vision.

Learning experts Gottfredson and Mosher (2010) categorized the five moments of need in learning. "Learning something new" (01) and "Learning more about something" (02) are among the moments of need in "formal learning". Knowledge transfer in formal learning takes place first and foremost through traditional methods like seminars, as well as e-learning in the form of online training courses.

Additionally, there are three moments of need that pertain to implementing what has been learned: "Using or remembering something" (03), "When a problem arises" (04) or "When something changes" (05).

The additional moments of need generally arise from the workflow. This is our starting point.

OUR WORKFLOW

We want you to maintain the overview in the strategy process and also have perspective. You will see both the wood and the trees. The basis of our Strategy-Frame® is the idea of learning at the moment of application. That is why we have structured our strategy process as a "workflow". The StrategyFrame® is designed in such a way that you can provide the "right" resources for your strategy work at the "right" time in the "right" amount of content in digestible form and on cascading instruction levels. For this reason, we have not geared and prepared this content along the lines of specialist topics, but instead we have classified them into specific individual tasks that you have to complete during the strategy process. Thus, you receive the relevant support right at your moment of need.

Our workflow comprises eight action steps you should take in the strategy process. We explain the necessity of each process step and give you a real instruction manual to work through with key questions, tips, examples, and tools. However, the workflow is not a one-way street. You will work through the StrategyFrame® several times across the workflow.

Process steps:
1. Plan
2. Analyze
3. Focus
4. Adapt
5. Cascade
6. Transform
7. Experiment
8. Adjust

STRATEGY DEVELOPMENT

2. ANALYZE

3. FOCUS

4. ADAPT

5. CASCADE

1. PLAN

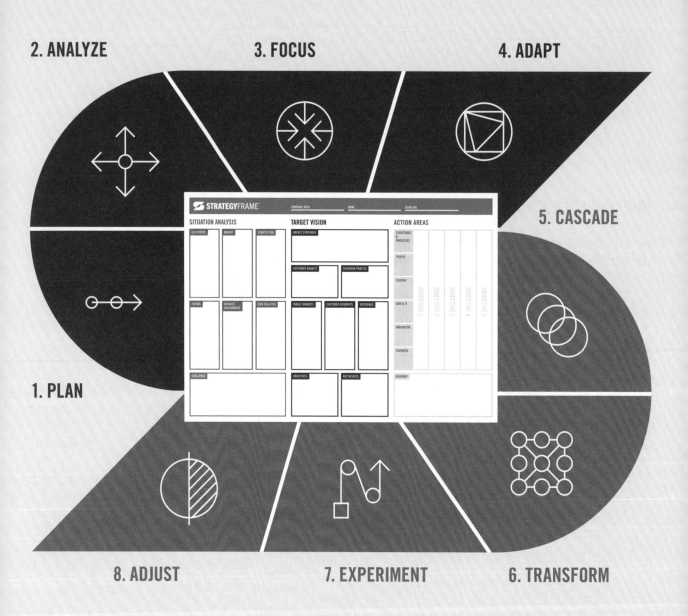

8. ADJUST

7. EXPERIMENT

6. TRANSFORM

STRATEGY EXECUTION

WORKFLOW

 ### 1. PLAN

Ask and answer the right questions to organize the process.

 ### 2. ANALYZE

Gather quantitative and qualitative data and analyze it with the right tools.

 ### 3. FOCUS

Reflect and discuss data and situation analysis in your team to make strategic decisions.

 ### 4. ADAPT

Develop tailored measures to adapt the organization to the target vision.

 ### 5. CASCADE

Properly stage and cascade the strategy across all levels.

 ### 6. TRANSFORM

Set up and start the transformation and accelerate change.

 ### 7. EXPERIMENT

Leverage unique skills and resources to create your growth engine for tomorrow and beyond.

 ### 8. ADJUST

Regularly challenge and sharpen the strategy.

"I LOVE IT WHEN A PLAN COMES TOGETHER."

Hannibal Smith, *The A-Team*

PLAN

PLAN YOUR STRATEGY PROCESS RIGHT

WHERE TO START

The first question is obvious: Can we do it ourselves? A strategy process that is going to succeed requires very good planning, and the participants have to enjoy doing it too. Without a well-thought-out plan and enjoyment of the process, the strategy process will quickly turn into a time-consuming, non-motivating event that feels like a burden, with little engagement among many participants and little to show as result. Then maybe it would be better to hire a consultancy firm after all? Will they let loose on us with "fancy" methods, take a sledgehammer to crack a nut? After countless rounds of interviews, will we be sticking Post-its onto boards with our colleagues in a series of workshops? Will we be overwhelmed in the end by an avalanche of number-crunching Excel sheets and tightly packed PowerPoint slides? And then what will we do with them? Unfortunately, this is frequently the reality companies face when they undertake strategy development!

Are you disheartened? Is it too much effort for too little return? And your nerves are rubbed raw on top of that? Are you now veering towards the anti-strategists' camp after all – just do what you can, only even better than before? Then a strategy won't be necessary? Or will it? We will support you on your journey of self-discovery. If you are not engaged, tweaking your future won't work. There is a lot to consider before you throw yourself into the work. But that does not mean it has to be deadly serious either.

Develop your own strategy

The next step is about the big picture: How do you plan a really good strategy process? How do you manage to make the process enjoyable alongside your day-to-day business? What questions do you have to answer before you start the process? We will provide you with a handbook to enable you to avoid problems that frequently arise in the development process or to think of solutions to them right from the start.

CALL A SPADE A SPADE

"In the beginning was the Word," the Gospel of John says. The word "strategy" is often avoided at the beginning of change processes for internal reasons, because it is considered to be unclear, overused or pretentious. People prefer to talk about an annual review, reorientation, or new mission. The word "mission" in particular has a ring of new departures to it and banks on the CEO as Chief Evangelist, the lead missionary to fire up markets and customers.

All too often, strategy is equated to or confused with formulating objectives, for example, "We want to increase our profits by 10 percent every year."

Come again? Why not by 50 percent? Or why increase at all?

But objectives are not a strategy, they are not implementable instructions – just desired results. Objectives stem from our ambitions, wishes and intentions. The crucial question in strategy development is not which objectives you want to aim for, but which challenges does your company face and what opportunities for development are available. Strategy isn't a bowl of cherries. It is your idea for how you can overcome these challenges and capitalize on the opportunities. The desired objectives are then derived from the challenges and opportunities.

This is your first assignment: Provide clarity. Call a spade a spade. Together with your management team and everyone who is supposed to contribute to the success of your strategy, develop a shared understanding of what strategy should be and what it should do. This brings us to the fundamental questions you will have to answer before starting any proposed change process:

#1: WHICH AREA OF YOUR COMPANY SHOULD THE STRATEGY BE DEVELOPED FOR?

FOR …
… THE ENTIRE COMPANY = CORPORATE STRATEGY:
The first and farthest-reaching area of application spans the entire company or all parts of a group of companies. We are then talking about corporate or group strategy. It determines where, when and how the company's resources are to be deployed to overcome the challenges that were identified and capitalize on available opportunities. Put simply, it is about defining and staking out the playing fields: Which markets and sectors does the company want to be active in? Which synergies can be created in a portfolio that consists of different products, services, and geographies?

… A BUSINESS AREA = BUSINESS AREA STRATEGY:
Larger companies generally have several business areas that require individual strategies within the overall context of a corporate strategy because of their distinctiveness. The business area strategy determines how the diagnosed challenges and opportunities should be tackled in the specific field of activity and how the business area wants to position itself against the competition.

… FOR FUNCTIONAL AREAS = FUNCTIONAL AREA STRATEGY:
The third organizational area of application pertains to functional areas of a company, such as procurement, production, marketing, distribution, financing, or personnel. In this area, the primary focus is on the integration of the individual functional areas to make a value contribution to the company's envisaged success.

Functional strategies cannot be established in isolation. Instead, they have to be coordinated with the overarching strategy areas "business area" and "company/ group" and contribute to their success. This can be seen from the current topics of "digital transformation" with the functional area IT as a center of gravity, or "sustainability", which particularly concerns the company areas of production, procurement, and logistics in manufacturing companies (for example, with the aim of reducing their "carbon footprint").

… REGIONS = GLOBAL, MULTINATIONAL OR LOCAL STRATEGY:

Alongside the organizational dimension of strategy, there is also the geographic area of application. Companies that operate internationally usually have a global corporate or group strategy into which the local business area strategies for different geographic markets are subsumed ("glocalization").

STORIES FROM THE FIELD

Sports and leisure goods manufacturer Adidas, for example, pursues this type of approach (2022).

The corporate strategy it calls "own the game" focuses on credibility, consumer experience and sustainability. It is designed to be implemented through continuous innovation and digitalization. The strategic markets, aka regions, are China, North America and EMEA. For each of these regions, Adidas has a "tailored approach that picks up on local trends" with the aim of "gaining market share in all three strategic markets."

It seems self-evident that the various business area, market, and functional strategies must be embedded at the corporate or group level. In practice, however, business area and function managers are increasingly finding themselves confronted with a lack of strategic considerations at the highest level. According to a study conducted by consultancy firm strategy& (2019), fewer than one-third of German companies have a clearly defined strategy that goes beyond general statements. If it is unclear how the deployment of resources pays into the company account and what the specific expectations from "above" entail, a certain arbitrariness ensues in the actions of all decision-makers. Not surprisingly, a silo mentality then spreads and prevents an integrative strategy that is oriented towards the challenges and opportunities.

#2: WHICH OVERARCHING OBJECTIVE ARE YOU PURSUING WITH YOUR STRATEGY AND WHICH IS YOUR FOCUS?

What are your strategic considerations really about? Should the current business model be questioned? Are we talking about a reorientation of core business? Should new business fields/business models be developed, or should a dual approach be pursued that combines both and drives them forward in parallel? Before you get into specific questions like these, it is important to understand what the strategic challenges are. Rumelt (2022) differentiates between three types of strategic challenges.

In the first type of challenge, the "choice challenge", you can understand the cause-and-effect connections and know alternative solutions. Your challenge comprises making the optimum decision amid conditions of uncertainty and not entirely quantifiable risks. Elon Musk had a production plant, a gigafactory, built in Berlin-Brandenburg to be able to cater to the anticipated rise in demand for e-vehicles in Germany and Europe. This meant that he entered into a longer-term commitment to this production location. Undoubtedly Musk and his strategists had alternative locations as well as alternative sizes of production plants on their analysis list. But Musk is known not to shy away from risk, and he therefore, unsurprisingly, chose the "no half measures" option.

1. Choice challenge

In the second type of challenge, the "engineering design challenge" there are no predefined or known alternative solutions from which the best is chosen by weighing up costs and benefits. A new solution is required. But at least there are examples or blueprints from previous experience or from observation of how others proceeded in similar situations. Then the nascent new approach can be tested against these models. In the past decades, German discount grocery retailers Aldi and Lidl have entered various new foreign markets. Although every national market has its peculiarities, these companies utilize tried and tested entry and expansion models and additionally used the new environments for experimenting (*Business Insider Deutschland*, 2018).

2. Engineering design challenge

The third type of challenge, the "gnarly design challenge", is particularly tricky, as it describes a situation that requires a decision where there are no known alternatives and no transferable action templates for the strategy that is sought. Interdependencies are unclear, relevant information is lacking, and available data can be interpreted in many different ways very differently. According to Kay and King (2020), there is "radical uncertainty":

3. Gnarly design challenge

"The result of our incomplete knowledge of the world, or about the connection between our present actions and their future outcomes. (…) There are things we do not know, and things we do not know that we do not know. And sometimes things we do know that are just not so."

Clarity about the type of strategic challenge will help you to define the "focus" of the strategy you wish to develop and conduct the right analyses. In our practical experience, the focus of strategies is generally on one of the following four areas:

PORTFOLIO:

☐ Growth (Invest)

☐ Stabilization (Hold)

☐ Shrinkage (Disinvest)

PRODUCTS/MARKETS:

☐ Market penetration

☐ Market development

☐ Product development

☐ Portfolio diversification

COMPETITIVE ADVANTAGES/MARKET COVERAGE:

☐ Cost leadership

☐ Product differentiation

☐ Concentration (entire market or niche)

MARKET BEHAVIOR:

☐ Attack

☐ Defense

☐ Win-win

PORTFOLIO (Corporate/group level)
(BCG Matrix, Henderson 1970): This is about the optimum allocation of your limited resources to the various corporate units. In which business fields do you want to grow? Growth requires investments. Where should you maintain your current market position? Where do you want to pare back your commitments to free up resources?

PRODUCTS/MARKETS (Business field/market level)
(Ansoff Matrix, Ansoff 1965): Do you want to penetrate existing markets with your current products (for example, by enhancing marketing measures) and increase your market share? Do you want to develop existing markets for your company with new products? Do you want to enter new markets with your current products and develop these markets for your company? Or do you want to diversify and establish new products in new markets?

POSITIONING AMONG THE COMPETITION (Business field/market level)
(Porter's Five Forces, Porter 1980): Do you want to stand out from your competitors in the selected business fields or markets by clear "differentiation" in terms of price and quality, or by "cost leadership"? Where should you direct your "concentration" – onto the entire market, or onto a niche?

MARKET BEHAVIOR (Market level)
Do you want to stage a frontal attack on the competition with the aim of market penetration and capture market share from them, as DHL attempted to do a few years ago in the USA against FedEx and UPS? Or do you want to act defensively instead, and not expose yourself on the entire market so that you do not trigger intense resistance from established market participants? Red Bull chose a defensive approach when it entered the US energy drink market to avoid counterstrikes from dominant firms Coca-Cola and Pepsi. Maybe you can also create win-win situations, for example, by increasing overall demand through your market development activities – and your competitors would profit from this as well.

Irrespective of whether your task is now to cut down your known alternatives (long list) to, for example, the best three (shortlist) to enable the optimum choice of a solution, or a complex challenge like growth in a saturated market environment: Clarify the type of strategic challenge with your management team, stake out your playing fields, and define the focus of your strategy.

#3: DO WE SPEAK THE SAME LANGUAGE AND DO WE MEAN THE SAME THING?

"The limits of my language mean the limits of my world."
Ludwig Wittgenstein, *Tractatus logico-philosophicus,* **1918**

If we want to develop and implement a strategy, we do not just need shared understanding at the content level. We must also speak a common language in our internal and external communication. Because language creates reality. That is one interpretation of the Wittgenstein quotation. A shared language, or rather, shared speech, creates closeness, commitment, and connection.

That is why you should not just call a spade a spade even before you set out on your strategy journey. You should also give your undertaking an inspirational description. In our daily business routines, the names given to strategies or strategy processes are usually not ever inventive, for example, "Strategy 2025", "Steel Strategy 20-30" or simply "Our Strategy". We have nothing against pragmatism and practicality unless it is just a mask for pure lack of imagination. But if a strategy is meant to really engage and inspire an organization, then a certain amount of emotionality and a strong message are needed inwardly as well as outwardly. So why not speak of "Bold Moves" instead of "Strategy 2025"? Or like Bertelsmann give your strategy a headline that emphasizes what it is about and what is at stake? - "Tomorrow is already here."

Language makes a difference

Language is not just decisive for naming and formulating a strategy. In fact, you should consider which language you wish to conduct your strategy process in. In many multinational companies, English is the working language. However, there are often no native English speakers among the participating decision-makers, or very few. Varying language skills among participants could distort the substance of the discussions, give native speakers the last word in interpreting terminology and change the balance of power in the strategy process. This problem is a major issue, even in international top teams at the corporate level. One of the authors of this book recently experienced this again in a strategy workshop with company area managers of an international corporation. English was agreed with the board of management as the workshop language. However, after a short time, it turned out that the language skills in the group varied too much to enable the participants to process terminology, content, and questions well and in a reasonable time to enable meaningful discussion. Even for participants with other native languages, switching to German was better than sticking with English. So, be sure to give some thought to language at an early stage and consider its effects on your strategy process.

#4: WHAT HALF-LIFE SHOULD YOUR STRATEGY HAVE?

The question of a period of relevance for a strategy is difficult to answer in today's "VUCA" world. The best answer is an economist's typical answer: it depends – on the company, the sector, and all the other factors that we want to include in our situation analysis. We do not know, and we cannot know, how **v**olatile, **u**ncertain, **c**omplex and **a**mbiguous the future will be. From our observations and analysis within companies and their respective business contexts, the half-life of corporate strategies emerges as a time corridor from about 3 to a maximum of 5 years.

Whether it is more or fewer years in the end: Strategy is not carved in stone. Depending on changes in market conditions and under pressure from competition, certain strategy elements (such as product strategy) can become obsolete faster than others (for example, operations strategy). That is why they should be reviewed at shorter intervals and require a more agile approach when new challenges or opportunities arise. The speed at which a corporate strategy can be adapted essentially depends on the size of the company. Experience shows that large companies require at least 2 to 3 years to develop a new strategy, implement it within the organization and make it tangible to customers.

At least 2 to 3 years

#5: WHAT BASIS WILL THE STRATEGY BE REORIENTED ON?

Do you have a corporate mission statement that anchors your strategy, that explains the company's purpose, defines its identity, determines the set of values and fundamental principles for your own actions and derives the vision and the work assignment for the organization? If not, then we recommend that you develop and communicate this type of self-perception before you turn your attention to the strategy work. A mission statement and a strategy should not be developed together or in parallel, since both the focus as well as the thought and communications methods are not identical.

Corporate mission statement

If you have a mission statement, you should review it because it will not always be transferable 1:1 onto a new strategy. To obtain the content required for the strategy process without running two processes in parallel and nonetheless achieving the best possible outcome, we work in practice with an "impact statement" – a promise to all stakeholders about how you plan to generate a positive effect with your company in your field of activity in the longer term (time frame: 5 to 10 years).

Our alternative: your impact statement

The impact statement is a blend of your passion, your company's strengths and the impetus of your economic engine. This is how it connects your "Why" (Sinek, 2019) to a big motivating objective that you want to bring to life (Sinek, 2011). You should position your impact statement in the target vision to generate momentum and give the blend a viable basis.

#6: WHAT IS THE TIME FRAME FOR YOUR STRATEGY PROCESS?

Before we go any further: Take your time on the strategy process. You won't develop a good strategy in 2 weeks. A sprint in the wrong direction will not take you any closer to your goal. Generally, there is a deadline for delivering your strategy message, for example, the annual shareholders' meeting, the supervisory or advisory board meeting, or the Financials press conference. Then this deadline will define the final date when at least the process of strategy development must be concluded.

If you want to conduct a robust and reliable situation analysis, you should plan for at least 4 to 8 weeks. This can also be achieved faster with high resource deployment and utilization of external consultants. It depends largely on the scope of the interview and data work required (collection, pooling, evaluation), because it won't work without solid quantitative and qualitative assessment. Excessive time pressure is counterproductive. It poses the risk of quick-fire decisions based on "gut feeling".

Once you have the results of the situation analysis, we recommend that you hold at least two workshops. The first workshop should take place with your top management team. The aim is to develop a shared understanding of the challenges and opportunities that were identified and draft a target vision that is compatible with your mission statement. Then, within 2 to 4 weeks of the first workshop, the second should be held with the wider management team to test the robustness of the target vision and to translate it into concrete action areas with measures.

Strategy development: 3 to 6 months

In total, you should allow for 3 to 6 months for strategy development. However, this step in the process should not take any longer because the world never stops turning. If it takes too long, your situation analysis could already be obsolete before you enter the phase of formulating objectives.

Strategy implementation: 1 year

The results of your strategy development must then be brought into the organization and processed there. This should be feasible within a year. Of course, the type and size of company, its developmental stage and the focus of the strategy must be taken into account here.

When you are implementing your strategy, ensure the following:

> • transparent communication – involve the implementers at an early stage and give them responsibility,
> • intelligent coordination of the various activities – they must be coherent, meaning aligned with each other and working towards the same goal, and
> • effective organization – define the roadmap and the milestones along the way, appoint a strategy process manager with executive authority.

A good strategy process requires a certain amount of agility and flexibility on the part of the strategy makers. Give your team space and time to maneuver.

#7: WHAT STRATEGY ARE YOU PURSUING AND HOW DOES A SHARED UNDERSTANDING OF THE STRATEGY EMERGE?

What elements are required to develop, communicate, and implement a complete strategy? There are multiple approaches, models, and methods you can use to develop an understanding of strategy and structure the strategy process. We are proponents of the KISS principle: "Keep it short and simple." That is why our StrategyFrame® comprises only three core elements: "Situation analysis", "Target vision" and "Action areas".

In our experience, it is important to get a panorama view that embeds these core elements into the overall context and acts as a platform for the joint work on content. When you have a view of the panorama, you can see the forest despite the trees. This makes it easier to reveal participants' expectations, attitudes and assumptions and clarify them.

The big picture

#8: WHO IS SPONSORING THE STRATEGY PROCESS?

Classic sponsors of corporate strategy are company board members or directors. In practice, a team approach has frequently been called for in recent times. Yes, strategy work is teamwork, but responsibility is not divisible. Ultimately, there has to be one person with overall responsibility, even if several people share responsibility for the strategy. Otherwise, there is a danger that particular interest of individual participants could put a brake on the process. Concentration onto a single person with overall responsibility provides clarity on who has the final say, particularly in situations that are critical to the success of the process, and who will take the rap for it in the end.

Boss

#9: WHO WILL ACT AS OPERATIONAL STRATEGY PROCESS MANAGER?

In many cases, a full-time strategist or personal assistant to the management board is responsible for the coordination and operational control of a strategy process. It does not necessarily have to be the most experienced colleague who leads the strategy process. Fresh, young minds can also be suited for this position if they are well networked and recognized within the company. However, more important than choosing the person is to fill the position at an early stage and maintain it, if possible, beyond the strategy development process to prevent a breakdown between strategy development and strategy implementation.

#10: WHO SHOULD BE INVOLVED IN THE STRATEGY PROCESS AND HELP DEVELOP IT?

Co-creation involves the active co-development of the strategy, including people outside the core management team, but particularly getting those people on board at an early stage who are going to implement and execute the strategy later. In our observation, the top executives don't like "meddling" and therefore especially do not want strategy development to be a participatory process. However, it can be very beneficial to tone down your own ego and not just allow collaboration outside the inner circle but actively canvass for it to gain valuable stimulus for the process and acceptance of the strategy later. The co-creators have empirical knowledge and contribute different perspectives that help you to question your own strategic deliberations. Really good executives can be recognized by the fact that it is not beneath their dignity to let others participate in the strategy development process.

Let us encourage you: When you choose co-creation, you send a strong message to your organization. By taking co-development measures, you make the people involved into co-owners and multipliers of the emerging strategy and thus promote acceptance and willingness to implement. (Co-)ownership creates obligation. However, you will also raise expectations among the participants. They may pursue their own agendas, causing unforeseeable team dynamics to develop. For this reason, despite all your enthusiasm for a co-creation process, you have to be sure to strike the right balance. Just because everyone is involved in the development does not necessarily mean that the resulting strategy will be more to their taste, or to everyone's taste. A democratic grass-roots vote is not a suitable vehicle for deciding on a new strategy. You must therefore stipulate the limits of the co-creation process in transparent and clear communication. The scope and intensity of the involvement will depend on the respective step in the strategy process. Undoubtedly, the first strategy workshop cannot be a staff meeting. In the first instance, top management has to reach common insights and considerations. At this altitude, the number of participants should be kept low. Our experience shows that the effectiveness of these meetings de-

People with an internal network and respect

Executives

clines significantly from eight to ten participants upwards. Then, in the second workshop, you can involve the broader management team with company area managers and, depending on the size of the company, where appropriate, even down to department head or team leader level. Independently of the co-creation process, there will also be opportunities during the ongoing process to integrate various stakeholder groups. For example, the viewpoints and expectations of internal and external stakeholders can be collected during qualitative interviews in the analysis phase.

#11: IS AN EXTERNAL CONSULTANT OR A SPARRING PARTNER REQUIRED? AND IF SO, WHO AND WHEN?

"Do-it-yourself"? Or do you want to take advantage of external support to develop and implement your new strategy? Do you have sufficient capacity within your company (staff, resources, time, capabilities and expertise) to execute the entire process, from analysis, through cascading right up to implementation – and adjustment?

Here comes a direct quote from a family-run company: "We can manage that ourselves despite limited capacities. Consultancies are expensive. After all, we're not a big corporation. In addition, consultants always just want to generate follow-up business." The role of consultants in strategy processes is increasingly changing. Of course, there are the big strategy consultancies that, when they receive a mandate from a large company, deploy legions of junior consultants for the core work from which experienced partners then develop customized strategies for the company executives. Naturally, expert work like this is expensive. And whether the strategy will succeed is anything but clear. Because as we know, the truth lies on the field when the game is on. By that time, the "hired guns" have long since moved on, involved in another project at another company. It is no surprise that particularly small and medium-sized companies have reservations and preconceptions about calling in external support. That is why highly specialized consultancies can increasingly score points here if they support the strategy process or parts of it as moderators, catalysts or sparring partners.

Good advice

If you are considering external support, you should reflect on what your company really needs in what area of the process. External moderation can help create fair discussion conditions and initiate constructive discussions free from arguments about justification and recriminations. Consultants and sparring partners can be the people who hold up the mirror you need before you and vocalize truths that no one from inside your company would dare to express. In addition, an overhead view from outside can give you new insights and impetus. And better still, it can be profitable.

#12: HOW WILL THE STRATEGY PROCESS BE COMMUNICATED?

The days of covert projects are over. It is a totally outdated idea that top management would sit alone behind closed doors hatching the new strategy and then present the new panacea with a "Hey presto" flourish to the organization. Get your team on board as early as possible in the strategy journey. Even if at the beginning it is merely by informing them that you are beginning deliberations in a select group of participants.

After this, the detailed work for your communication begins. Define the communication channels. Make the various steps in the planned strategy process transparent. Explain the procedure and the time and resource expenditure you envisage. Present the process roadmap. Empower people outside the management team as well to act as multipliers or strategy ambassadors within the organization. The main objective here is to communicate interim results and progress in the process.

Even at the risk of repeating ourselves, we must emphasize here: Communication is the key to the success of strategy processes. That is not a management platitude but insight based on experience. Philosopher Hans Jonas (1992) summed it up in a nutshell: "Stand firm in the conviction that how you think, what you think, what you say and how you disseminate ideas in mutual communication makes a difference to the way of things."

The "way of things" in this book is the "process".

Communication is a critical
success factor

"OUR GOALS CAN ONLY BE REACHED THROUGH A VEHICLE OF A PLAN, (...). THERE IS NO OTHER ROUTE TO SUCCESS."

Pablo Picasso, Spanish artist

PLAN

Where do most strategy processes fail? In their implementation? Maybe. But how many processes don't even make it that far because they are abandoned already at the development stage, because the understanding of strategy varies widely from person to person, or because the conditions for an organized strategy process were not created? You can do better! Try to answer as many questions as possible from the beginning. Make assumptions, expectations, and misgivings explicit so that you can gain clarity for the initial steps of the process.

KEY QUESTIONS:

1. ☐ Which area of your company should the strategy be developed for?

2. ☐ Which overarching aim are you pursuing with the strategy? What is your primary focus?

3. ☐ Do we speak the same language, and do we mean the same thing?

4. ☐ What half-life should your strategy have?

5. ☐ On what basis is the strategy being reoriented?

6. ☐ What is the time frame for your strategy process?

7. ☐ What strategic framework are you applying and how will a shared understanding of strategy emerge?

8. ☐ Who is the sponsor of the strategy process?

9. ☐ Who is acting as operational manager of the strategy process?

10. ☐ Who must be involved in the strategy process and co-develop it?

11. ☐ Is an external consultant or sparring partner required? And if so, who and when?

12. ☐ How will the strategy process be communicated?

INSTRUCTIONS

Work through the questions together in a smaller group. At least the sponsors and the strategy process manager should be present. The objective is to develop a shared understanding of the process ahead. Even if you cannot answer all the questions yet, exchange ideas on potential options and alternatives. Do not let anything fall by the wayside.

ASSUMPTIONS

TO KEY QUESTIONS

1. **Organizational area of applicability:** _____

   Regional area of applicability: _____

2. **Focus of the strategy:** _____

3. **Leading language of the process:** _____

   Description of the process: _____

   Name of the process: _____

4. **Time frame for the strategy: 20** ____

5. **What can be used as a basis?**   Mission statement ☐   Vision ☐   Purpose ☐   Why ☐   BHAG ☐

6. **Initial presentation of the strategy you developed:** ___.___._____

   Work date Strategy Workshop I (Top team): ___.___._____

   Work date Strategy Workshop II (Broader management team): ___.___._____

7. **Selected process or methodological model:** _____

8. **Sponsor of the strategy process:** _____

9. **Strategy process manager:** _____

10. **People (groups) to involve:** _____

    _____

    _____

    Circle of participants

STRATEGY WORKSHOP I:	STRATEGY WORKSHOP II:
_____	_____
_____	_____
_____	_____

11. **Potential consultants, moderators or sparring partners for the process, specific process steps or modules:**

    _____

    _____

12. **First milestones for communicating the strategy process:**

Date	Content	Target group	Format	Channel
___.___.____	_____	_____	_____	_____
___.___.____	_____	_____	_____	_____
___.___.____	_____	_____	_____	_____

ROADMAP I

COMPANY AREA _____

	WEEK ___ from ___.___.___ to ___.___.___	WEEK ___ from ___.___.___ to ___.___.___	WEEK ___ from ___.___.___ to ___.___.___	WEEK ___ from ___.___.___ to ___.___.___
PLAN				
PLANNING MEETING	☐☐☐☐☐	☐☐☐☐☐	☐☐☐☐☐	☐☐☐☐☐
KICK-OFF MEETING	☐☐☐☐☐	☐☐☐☐☐	☐☐☐☐☐	☐☐☐☐☐
MANAGEMENT CIRCLE	☐☐☐☐☐	☐☐☐☐☐	☐☐☐☐☐	☐☐☐☐☐
REGULAR MEETING	☐☐☐☐☐	☐☐☐☐☐	☐☐☐☐☐	☐☐☐☐☐
ANALYZE				
COLLECT QUANTITATIVE DATA	☐☐☐☐☐	☐☐☐☐☐	☐☐☐☐☐	☐☐☐☐☐
CONDUCT EXPLORATIVE INTERVIEWS	☐☐☐☐☐	☐☐☐☐☐	☐☐☐☐☐	☐☐☐☐☐
ANALYZE THE QUANTITATIVE AND QUALITATIVE DATA	☐☐☐☐☐	☐☐☐☐☐	☐☐☐☐☐	☐☐☐☐☐
FOCUS				
STRATEGY WORKSHOP I	☐☐☐☐☐	☐☐☐☐☐	☐☐☐☐☐	☐☐☐☐☐
ADAPT				
STRATEGY WORKSHOP II	☐☐☐☐☐	☐☐☐☐☐	☐☐☐☐☐	☐☐☐☐☐
INITIAL COMMUNICATION	☐☐☐☐☐	☐☐☐☐☐	☐☐☐☐☐	☐☐☐☐☐
SUPPORTING COMMUNICATION	☐☐☐☐☐	☐☐☐☐☐	☐☐☐☐☐	☐☐☐☐☐
INTRODUCE THE STRATEGYFRAME®	☐☐☐☐☐	☐☐☐☐☐	☐☐☐☐☐	☐☐☐☐☐
STRATEGY IMPLEMENTATION				
PROCESS STEP 5–8	☐☐☐☐☐	☐☐☐☐☐	☐☐☐☐☐	☐☐☐☐☐

NAME _____   DATE _____

WEEK ___ from ___.___.___ to ___.___.___	WEEK ___ from ___.___.___ to ___.___.___	Q ___ from ___.___.___ to ___.___.___	Q ___ from ___.___.___ to ___.___.___	NOTES

"HOWEVER BEAUTIFUL THE STRATEGY, YOU SHOULD OCCASIONALLY LOOK AT THE RESULTS."

Winston Churchill, British statesman

ANALYZE

WHERE YOU ARE

FIGURES, DATA, FACTS

Facing the truth

Before you formulate the objectives that are aligned to the challenges and opportunities and start looking for the best ways to get there, you have to understand where your company stands today, how you got there, and how your journey could continue. As Willie Pietersen (2001), a grand master of strategy, teaches us: "The starting point of any strategy is a great situation analysis. (...) Intelligence precedes operations." Another grand master, Richard Rumelt (2022), holds a similar opinion: "The key steps in dealing with a strategic challenge are a diagnosis of the situation – a comprehension of 'what's going on here,' finding the crux, and then creating reasonable action responses."

Thus, in the situation analysis, we are talking about the "Where do we stand?" It is a systematic and logically stringent approach which can be metaphorically described as a combination of Albert Einstein and Charles Darwin. In this analogy, Einstein's famous formula, $E = mc2$, serves as a metaphor for investigating the interdependencies among your company's fields of activity. To do this, you and your team must first collate data and facts on these fields of activity, evaluate them and decide which information is relevant for answering the critical questions ahead, and which is not. The questions could be, for example: What are the success factors in your selected areas? What are the reasons for the discrepancies between market share and profitability? How are our relationships with customers, suppliers, and other interested parties in comparison with our competitors? Do the conclusions from the analysis of the facts and the data concur with our subjective observations and experience in the fields of activity?

Darwin examined the evolution of living beings, the emergence of biodiversity and the extinction of species from a historical perspective. He delivered explanations for reproduction, adaptation, mutation, and the survival of the most adaptable. His evolutionary research approach can act as a metaphor for the necessity to recognize development patterns and trends and comprehend their significance for our own existence. How and why is our present different from the past? How could tomorrow differ from today, and why? To throw a phrase into the mix that owes its existence to the Covid-19 pandemic: What will be the next "new normal"?

Your company and its "own realities" will be the core focus of the situation analysis: How profitable are we? How could we grow? Normally, your company will be embedded in a specific industry or sector. It will have resources and capabilities that you must combine intelligently and efficiently to make your company distinguishable from the competition.

YOUR COMPANY'S STRATEGIC ENVIRONMENT

There are four general forces impacting your company. On the one hand, there is the "market forces" field. Markets are not synonymous with industries or sectors. An industry like, for example, the chemical industry has a multitude of product markets in different geographies. And a market like the car market is served by market participants from various industries (automotive manufacturers, dealerships, insurance companies, banks). Markets emerge from demarcating definitions across two dimensions: Similarity of products to satisfy identical customer requirements and geographic location of the offering.

Market

On the market level, the forces of supply and demand affect your company. The "competition" force field lies on the supply side. Companies that offer comparable products from a customer's point of view are in competition with each other. Coca-Cola and Pepsi's best-known products are carbonated, sugary beverages. They are sold worldwide. Both companies are direct competitors globally, regionally, and locally. Likewise, Fritz-kola from Hamburg is also a direct competitor, but only in a small number of countries.

Competition

Is mineral water supplier Perrier also a direct competitor? That depends on how we define the market. It depends most of all on the "customers" force field, on their requirements and preferences. If customers are looking for a thirst-quenching, refreshing drink, independent of sugar content, then Perrier and all other mineral water producers will become direct competitors of Coca-Cola and Pepsi.

Customers

Additionally, your company is subject to overarching forces on the macro level in the "broader environment". These are exogenous factors on the macroeconomic or international level which significantly impact your actions (for example, state regulation, company taxation, trade policy). On top of these, there are the "trends", triggered for example, by overriding and enduring technological, socioeconomic or cultural developments that lead to far-reaching changes in the legacy playing fields or open up new playing fields.

Broader environment & Trends

To reach valid insights and viable conclusions, the situation analysis must create transparency. In short: Leave no stone unturned, do not regard anything as a random outlier. This is the only way to understand interdependencies. Then, instead of treating the symptoms, you can treat the causes specifically. By the end of the situation analysis, you have gained an understanding of how relevant your company is in its current fields of activity and how it can remain relevant for the future.

STRATEGYFRAME®

COMPANY AREA

SITUATION ANALYSIS

CUSTOMERS	MARKET	COMPETITION

TRENDS	BROADER ENVIRONMENT	OWN REALITIES

CHALLENGE

TARGET VISION

IMPACT STATEMENT

CUSTOMER BENEFIT

TARGET MARKETS	CUSTOMER SEGMENTS

OBJECTIVES

NAME

DEADLINE

ACTION AREAS

STRUCTURES &
PROCESSES

PEOPLE

SUPERIOR PROFITS

CULTURE

OFFERINGS

DATA & IT

INNOVATION

PARTNERS

KEY RESULTS   ROADMAP

STRATEGY KICK-OFF MEETING

Together, we see more. How you set up your strategy process will send a powerful signal for its implementation. Be brave. Put a team together that is willing and able to adopt different perspectives and voice opposition – on merit and not based on personal vanities.

In your kick-off meeting, you should lay a foundation of trust for the joint strategy work. Always show your hand. Clarify fundamental opinions and attitudes, explain the envisaged procedure and the content of the various steps that you want to take together, and be open to a critical discussion.

AGENDA (PROPOSAL):

1. **Check-in: Formulate questions to all participants**
   (Example: Why do we need a strategy process?)

2. **Objective: Clarify the management team's expectations**

3. **Methodology:**
   - **Explain the StrategyFrame®**
   - **Introduce the key questions for each module of the situation analysis and add to them if necessary**
   - **Suggest potential analysis tools (see individual modules)**

4. **Status quo (optional): Present prior estimate of data pool for the individual modules in a traffic-light system**

5. **Organization:**
   - **Clarify roles in the process**
   - **Procedure: Present the schedule and agree on it**
   - **Agree on IT systems for data storage and project management**

6. **Quantitative analyses: Appoint executives responsible for collecting and analyzing the quantitative data for the individual modules**

7. **Define the forms of qualitative analyses**
   (For example, for exploratory interviews with customers, stakeholders, and the management team, name these persons specifically)

8. **Check-out: Formulate questions to all participants**
   (Example: What contribution can I make to the process?)

INSTRUCTIONS

Use the Socratic method of structured dialog. Key questions will lead into the topics for discussion. The answers will serve as a starting point for more in-depth questions, like for example: "Why do you see it like that?" or "What are the assumptions underlying your answer?" You should question the new answers together. Repeat the sequence: "Question – query – challenge" until you have reached a shared insight.

1. Formulate the key questions
2. Amalgamate the quantitative and qualitative data
3. Analyze and discuss
4. Derive key insights

TIP

Here are five golden rules:

1. Make a diagnosis, not just an overview of the symptoms. You want to find out the cause of results and their consequences. Separate the important from the unimportant.
2. Trends tell a story; snapshots are an image of a moment in time without a "Why?" and "What comes after that?" When you are analyzing your results, look for connected chronological sequences, map these as possible trends and find the common stories behind them.
3. Keep it short and simple (KISS)! Don't overcomplicate results. Searching for meaning requires crystal-clear answers. Simplicity is not a shortcut; it is a virtue, and it is hard work.
4. Avoid overused phrases or jargon! Formulate your thoughts and insights in such a way even outsiders will understand them. Speak your customers' language instead of corporate gibberish.
5. Reaching a consensus is the wrong objective: The best ideas should prevail, not the "average" or the lowest common denominator.

CAUTION

You should select your management team so that it is big enough to have diversity, but it should not be too big either to keep the complexity of agreement low. In our experience, a core team with five to six people, including the strategy process manager, works well. The question of who should be on the team often depends decisively, alongside professional competence and position, on internal culture and politics. Of course, you can also define a larger circle, for example, because you want to give someone their first chance to prove themselves, or because you would like to include people who can act as multipliers to ensure acceptance for your strategy process among the workforce. However, you should not go beyond 10 to 12 participants.

MODULES

	COLLECT DATA	ANALYZE DATA	EXTERNAL REQUIREMENTS	DATA SUPPLIER/ CONSULTANT
CUSTOMERS	Name	Name	Yes ☐ No ☐	Consultant's/Supplier's name
MARKET	Name	Name	Yes ☐ No ☐	Consultant's/Supplier's name
COMPETITION	Name	Name	Yes ☐ No ☐	Consultant's/Supplier's name
TRENDS	Name	Name	Yes ☐ No ☐	Consultant's/Supplier's name
BROADER ENVIRONMENT	Name	Name	Yes ☐ No ☐	Consultant's/Supplier's name
OWN REALITIES	Name	Name	Yes ☐ No ☐	Consultant's/Supplier's name

STRATEGY INTERVIEWS

GET QUALITATIVE INSIGHTS

A major challenge for strategy developers lies in reaching a shared understanding of the strategy process among the management team. Without such an understanding it will be difficult to make meaningful strategic decisions. The interviews make a decisive contribution to achieving this goal because the respondents' diverging perspectives, assumptions and sensitivities become visible and can be clarified.

If you don't ask, you don't want to know. But if you do ask, you will get answers from the situation analysis. A successful situation analysis will highlight what your company has achieved up to the present day, where its strengths lie, and which areas need work. As a commercial enterprise, your work has to be based on figures and you have to keep your "key performance indicators" in your sights. Hence your situation analysis won't work without figures. That is why a key portion of the results of your situation analysis will be quantitative.

Perception complements the figures

However, if spreadsheets are presented and screens are filled with rows of numbers, people can easily become unable to see the wood for the trees. That is why it is important, in our experience, to illustrate a company's internal and external realities with qualitative instruments as well as, for example, with exploratory interviews.

SEMI-STRUCTURED EXPLORATORY INTERVIEWS

The exploratory interview is a form of qualitative survey. It can be held personally, orally and in person or virtually. Thus, apart from what is said, the interviewee's non-verbal communication can also be observed. You should choose a dialog-oriented discussion format since a process that is limited to a question-and-answer sequence could be experienced by the interviewees as an "interrogation" – especially when there are sensitive questions involved.

We also recommend that you structure the discussion beforehand based on key questions on the topics in the situation analysis that you would like to address – but without planning the entire discussion minutely. The benefit of a "semi-structured interview" like this is that the interviewees see themselves as dialog partners and you are giving them intellectual space to respond, ask their own questions and discuss. It is important to emphasize to the interviewees that the object of the interview is not to substantiate or refute existing hypotheses on the quantitative results. Instead, the aim is to gather as many impressions, opinions, attitudes, or suggestions as time-efficiently as possible. The interviewees' subjective perceptions can then be used on the one hand to gain insights that permit better comprehension of the quantitative results. On the other hand, causal relationships and development patterns can emerge over and above the interviews that cannot be derived from the quantitative data on its own.

VOLUNTARY, ANONYMOUS, OPEN

But now who should interview whom to gain the best possible insights? The first question to answer is who should be interviewed because you might possibly have some surveys already, for example, from customers. Basically, you should be aiming to get a 360° view – but maybe this is not feasible because of budget or time factors. In that case, we suggest that you prioritize from inside to outside:

1. Internal key people
   (participating management team before other groups of people)
2. Important internal or external stakeholders
3. Active customers and non-customers
4. External experts

Potential interview groups

After the key people in the organization as well as the owners and employees, then come the external stakeholders, first and foremost the customers, and other externals.

You should schedule around 6 to 8 weeks for a solid exploratory survey, including analysis – irrespective of the number of interviewees and the number of interviewers. This brings us to two central, but often conflicting, topics: Who should conduct the interviews? And how do we ensure that the people being interviewed are not evasive, but are open and share their unfiltered opinions?

Independent third-party viewpoint is helpful

The qualitative analysis is time-consuming, but it can make a decisive difference in achieving significant advances in insight. You will gain an understanding of the psyche of the people in your company, whether they are executives, regular employees, or shareholders, and you get insight into what they think about the present state and future of your company, what expectations and needs they have. The same applies to your customers and their expectations, wishes, and preferences. In brief: As long as people are still responsible for strategy, the additional expenditure for a survey is worthwhile. Our recommendation: Question, query, and challenge. It pays off.

STRATEGY INTERVIEWS

On the following worksheets we have compiled all the information you need to conduct your strategy interviews successfully. Apart from specifying the procedure, tips and comments, we also propose potential key questions across the entire StrategyFrame® in the core module Situation Analysis.

INSTRUCTIONS:

1. **Prepare the interviews:**
   - **Define interview groups**
   - **Prepare a questionnaire with key questions**
   - **Invite the interview participants and arrange interview times**

2. **Conduct the interviews (60 to 90 minutes)**
   - **Short presentation**
   - **Start digital recording**
   - **Steer the interview using key questions**

3. **Evaluate the interviews**
   - **Transcribe the recorded interviews**
   - **Form clusters along the StrategyFrame®**
   - **Code the statements**
   - **Mark illustrative quotes**

4. **Incorporate insights into the modules of the situation analysis**
   - **Add observations to each module with illustrative quotes**

TIP

- Number of interviews: 10 to max. 35 (if you have more interviews, the time and effort required for evaluation rises enormously, but the insights gained do not)
- Duration of each interview: at least 45 to max. 90 mins.
- Interviews per day: no more than 3
- Ask open questions: This enables a discussion to develop
- Query, query, query: Use simple query words like "why", to dig deeper
- Be an active listener
- Code systematically: Use software for the repetitive work

CAUTION

If you wish to interview employees in your company, you should clarify whether you need approval from your company union or works council (if you have one) to do this. When we conduct our internal surveys in the strategy process, we try to stay on the current management levels. You cannot force anyone to take part in a survey or to give their permission to make their opinion public. Voluntary participation and guaranteed anonymity are fundamental prerequisites for openness among the interviewees. If there is no willingness to be open among the interviewees, you will not get all the information you need from them for your strategy process.

Although you can certainly contact external stakeholders independently, it will be difficult to conduct a survey neutrally within your own company and evaluate it objectively – irrespective of how good your company culture and mutual trust are (or are perceived to be).

For these reasons, it totally makes sense to call in external support here to conduct the survey impartially, ensure anonymous evaluation of the results and communicate them credibly.

INTERVIEW PARTICIPANTS

STAKEHOLDER GROUP	LAST NAME/ FIRST NAME	FUNCTION	COMPANY	PLANNING
				invited ☐ scheduled ___ . ___ . _____ ___ : ___ am/pm conducted ☐
				invited ☐ scheduled ___ . ___ . _____ ___ : ___ am/pm conducted ☐
				invited ☐ scheduled ___ . ___ . _____ ___ : ___ am/pm conducted ☐
				invited ☐ scheduled ___ . ___ . _____ ___ : ___ am/pm conducted ☐
				invited ☐ scheduled ___ . ___ . _____ ___ : ___ am/pm conducted ☐
				invited ☐ scheduled ___ . ___ . _____ ___ : ___ am/pm conducted ☐

QUESTIONNAIRE

The following elements should help you draft a questionnaire that is adapted to your purposes to conduct semi-structured interviews. Conduct the interviews in person or digitally as dialog-based meetings by working through the key questions. Your focus should be on letting your interview partner speak freely and openly. Your priority will be to listen. Your key questions will provide the thematic framework. They might have to be adapted for the various stakeholder groups.

INSTRUCTIONS:

The following basic ground rules apply
to the interviews:

1. A clearly defined time frame
   (45 – 90 minutes is ideal)
2. The interviewer's openness and neutrality
3. Strict preservation of anonymity of results
4. Destruction of all recordings after evaluation

Why are we conducting this interview?
We would like to know ...

... where does our company stand today?
... how is our environment developing?
... what is our biggest challenge?
... how does our company plan
    to win the competition for customers?
... how will we implement our strategy?

WHAT WILL HAPPEN TO THE RESULTS?

The insights gained will be incorporated into the development of your future strategy.

SELECTION OF KEY QUESTIONS

SELECTION OF POTENTIAL KEY QUESTIONS

Customer requirements & expectations

- What are the trends in customer expectations? What is different today compared to yesterday? What will be different tomorrow compared to today?
- Can customers be segmented in a meaningful way? Which segments will we address? Which will we not address?
- What does our target customers' hierarchy of requirements look like (meaning: what is most important to them)?
- How well do we and the competition fulfil these requirements today?

Market conditions & competition

- How would you describe the general development of the focus markets? Where do you see the greatest potential for today and tomorrow?
- Who are our current competitors?
- How do our current competitors serve the respective market? How effective are they in our customers' eyes compared to us?
- How profitable are we compared to our major competitors? What are the main drivers of their earnings performance?
- Who are potential competitors and what unique benefits can they offer? Who poses the greatest danger, and why?

The new rules for success

- Which trends are the most important for the structure and development of our sector/industry? What are their causes and further implications?
- How are these trends changing the rules of the game and the factors for success?
- What threats do these trends pose to our profitability? What opportunities do they open up?

What else influences us …
What has an effect on our business from our environment with regard to:

- Macroeconomic developments
- Social habits and attitudes
- Geopolitics
- Demographics
- Legal and regulatory developments

Own reality

- How does the five-year trend in our key performance figures look like? What conclusions can we draw?
- Where are we making money, and where aren't we?
- Which of our product ranges are winning, and which are losing? Why?
- What are our major strengths that we can use as competitive advantages?
- What are our major weaknesses that are standing in the way of better performance?

What makes the difference

- What will we do differently or better than the competition to offer our target customers more value added?
- If you had three wishes, what would you change?

Future

- Where do you see the company in 5 years?

Conclusion

- Do you have any additional comments or pointers?

CUSTOMERS

PUT CUSTOMERS FIRST

In our digital times, a customer-centered approach is considered the sole deciding factor for a company to succeed in business. This is so easy to say, write and promise – but has not yet found its way into many companies' reality. Because customer centricity requires a fundamental change of perspective – and thus a shift from navel-gazing at your own company to a consistent orientation to customers and their requirements.

Companies that are less exposed to competition find it particularly hard to maintain a customer perspective and orientation. Sheer product availability with consistent product quality is still an unbeatable reason for customers to remain loyal, even if companies do not treat them well. But their luxurious position of strength with respect to customers is crumbling. Unexpected external shocks like the Covid-19 pandemic and the gas crisis due to the Russian aggression in Ukraine have now reached the Isles of the Blest too. Supply disruptions, production bottlenecks and rising inflation are changing customer requirements, customer preferences and willingness to pay. The demand side is moving, but the supply side is at a standstill and licking its wounds. Many companies have already had to bid farewell to the glory days of "everything goes".

When you have customer centricity, you attune yourself lock, stock and barrel to identifying and satisfying your customers' needs. You develop new products, services, or even new business models from a customer perspective. This approach affects all areas of a company and therefore is of considerable significance, if not to say decisive importance, for your corporate strategy.

When you are going through your strategic considerations, you must know what challenges and opportunities exist on your demand side. Who are "your" customers, both current and potential, how do they behave, what do they need, what are their pain points, and what are their preferences? Who are your non-customers, and why?

Get the customer in your sights

CLOSE PROXIMITY TO CUSTOMERS

"We know our customers very well, and we know what they need." That is awesome but unfortunately rarely true. Our experience from various projects with companies shows: When we ask when someone from the management team last visited a customer and was able to watch them using the company's product(s), we are usually met with deafening silence.

Let us take a closer look at some of the myths about analyzing customers. Test yourself on these honestly:

#1: CUSTOMERS' REQUIREMENTS ARE CHANGING WAY TOO FAST

Customers' requirements change, there is no question about that. Fulfilled requirements disappear, new requirements emerge, preferences shift focus. Established customers with familiar preferences leave, new customers with different expectations and preferences come on board. How fast this happens is a different question because it takes some time before people change their behaviors. This is how cheap meat products can still sell well even in boom times for healthy nutrition and meat substitute products.

STORIES FROM THE FIELD

The vegetarian curried sausage delivers a good example. When car maker VW replaced the classic curried sausage with a vegetarian and a vegan version in its company canteen in the company's headquarters in Wolfsburg in 2021, the outcry to save the curried sausage was huge in social media across Germany – even coming from a former German chancellor.

However, the fact that the meat version is on offer in 30 of the automotive manufacturer's other company canteens in Wolfsburg alone, and that every year around 7 million (2019) portions of the cult sausage leave the group's own butcher's shop, speaks for itself. In addition, the original version of the "curry bockwurst" can be bought by specialist retailers under the product number "199 398 5000 A" and by consumers in various retail chains. Like the Germans' love of cash, the meat bockwurst will still have its fans for a long time to come, even if vegetarian success stories like Rügenwalder Mühle address new requirements specifically and highly successfully.

#2: CUSTOMERS DO NOT KNOW THEIR OWN REQUIREMENTS

All too often, executives and particularly sales professionals can be heard saying that customers do not know their own requirements at all. What they mean is: We know better what customers really want and need and develop new targeted products accordingly. To illustrate this, product innovations like Apple's iPod and iPhone, which Steve Jobs pushed onto the market, are often happily rolled out. But even these top sellers are based on previously known and clear consumer requirements (for example, Sony's Walkman as a portable miniature cassette player).

#3: CUSTOMERS CANNOT ARTICULATE THEIR REQUIREMENTS

That is not true. Or at least, as Nobel Prize winner Paul Samuelson (1938) argues in his "revealed preferences theory", the ultimate buying decision reveals the customers' preferences for the goods they just purchased. However, that means that we do not yet know what tipped the scales in favor of the purchase in the end (the price, suitable product features, the immediate availability, or something else). But even if customers do not articulate their requirements directly, they can be observed in certain circumstances.

When you conduct the situation analysis it makes sense to use various methods to find out something about customers' requirements as well as their prioritization and change. Field tests like customer shadowing or testing out prototypes in design thinking processes are common methods for identifying customer requirements. At the same time, you should investigate how your competitors' products satisfy these customer requirements.

"THE CUSTOMER PERCEPTION IS YOUR REALITY."

Kate Zabriskie, President, Business Training Works

CUSTOMERS

Do you understand your customers' most important requirements and expectations? Understanding always starts with listening and looking! There are many ways to reach a goal. Depending on your existing data pool, budget, and deadline, you should observe or interview your customers, or consult external analysts. On this point, experience shows: The more insights you get into your customers' most visceral expectations and experiences, the better for your understanding. Our recommendation: Leave your desk now and again and head out to the front lines, to your customers.

KEY QUESTIONS:

1. Which customer segments are relevant for us?

2. Which customers do we want to address, and which don't we?

3. How have our customers' demands and requirements changed from yesterday to today? How will they change from today to tomorrow?

4. Which requirements are most important to our target customers?

5. How well do we fulfill these requirements today?

6. How well do our competitors fulfill these requirements today?

COLLECT THE DATA

Prioritize various types of analysis by time and effort/difficulty:

Our recommendations:
- Accessible external and internal "studies"
- "Exploratory interviews" with selected customers and non-customers
- Creation of "personas" combined with external methods for validating hypotheses

Other:
- Use "customer shadowing" to observe customers using the products and services
- Illustrate the customer journey with "customer journey maps"
- Directed discussion by "focus group interviews"
- Investigate customer satisfaction using the "net promoter score" (NPS)
- Use "conjoint analysis" to identify customer preferences

TIP

To identify your customers' requirements better, observe three potential requirement dimensions for your customers and describe these briefly in your own words:

1. **Tasks:** Which tasks does the customer want to complete in their work or in their daily life?

2. **Problems:** Which risks, bad results or obstacles arise when the customer completes the task?

3. **Benefit:** Which specific value added would the customer like to achieve by completing this task?

ANALYZE THE DATA

Based on the results of your survey, draw up a list of your customers' requirements by customer segment. Restrict the requirements to the top 10 and prioritize them. Categorize the requirements by type of requirement (task, problem, benefit). Finally, make an estimate for how well your company and the competitors fulfil the requirements today:

+ = requirement fulfilled

0 = requirement partially fulfilled

– = requirement not fulfilled

CAUTION

Observing customers is not a desk job. Leave the office and meet your customers in their habitat. For your customer analyses draw on the knowledge, experiences and insights of your employees from various functional areas, such as Marketing, Sales or Customer Service. You can evaluate the results in the first Strategy Workshop.

SOURCES

ANALYSIS

CUSTOMER SEGMENT:

IMPORTANCE	CUSTOMER NEEDS	TYPE	US	COMPETITION

QUALITATIVE OBSERVATIONS

CUSTOMERS

FORMULATE INSIGHTS

INSTRUCTIONS

Draw your key insights from analyzing customer requirements. Formulate them in short and snappy understandable language as preparation for the first strategy workshop. You should regard the formulation as a coherent story which you will tell later as the basis of your strategic decisions. You can then draft the ultimate formulations with your team in the workshop.

EXAMPLES

- Customers increasingly expect more individualization in products.
- The days of a "one-stop shop" with a full product range are gone.
- Rising customer expectations regarding sustainability are clashing with increasing price pressure on the part of OEMs.
- B2B customers are expanding their value chains by handling our core business themselves.

MARKET

IDENTIFY RELEVANT MARKETS

"The grass is always greener in the neighbor's garden, but the weeds grow better in our own."
Hans-Jürgen Quadbeck-Seeger, German chemist

How well do you know the playing field your company is playing on? How will it develop in the future? Does it still offer your company sufficient growth potential, or are there potentially more attractive opportunities for your company on other playing fields?

Even if you or your colleagues on your management team believe we know the company's playing field like the back of your hand, you should take a step back and cast a fresh, impartial look at the arena of markets and market segments. To ensure you avoid errors of assessment because of cognitive distortions (such as confirmation bias which provokes one-sided data selection) we recommend that you additionally request a neutral party to provide an independent observation.

What you need for the strategic evaluation of your arena is on the one hand an overall picture of the markets and market segments your company addresses already, and on the other hand you should understand the development to date and the potential for the future of every current playing field and potential new fields of activity.

Your task is to evaluate the current size of the market, market attractiveness, which must be measured by the opportunities for profit and are influenced by the type and intensity of the competition. You should answer the following questions:

Your key questions

1. How big is the market?
2. How is the market developing?
3. How big is the theoretical market potential?

ON 1: DETERMINE MARKET SIZE

Before we can determine the size of a market, the market as well as any sub-markets and product segments must be defined. The sector boundary can be used as a starting point. The sector describes companies that offer similar products and services, like for example, trading, construction, or the health sector.

Within every sector there are subgroups. For trading, for example, we find the subgroups of retail, wholesale, specialized trade, or food retail. Publicly accessible sources for sectoral data are available for example, from the Federal Statistics Office for Germany and Eurostat at the EU level. There are also several commercial data providers which can prepare data for you on the number of providers, revenues, unit sales or customer preferences. Of course, you can also have studies conducted on the volume and potential of relevant product-specific and geographic market segments.

Get yourself a detailed insight into your relevant market.

ON #2: CHECK THE MARKET DYNAMICS

When you look at the market development up to today, your task is to gain a better understanding of the market dynamics. What is the condition of the relevant focus market on which you are operating? How have supply and demand developed? Is the market growing, is it saturated, or is it even shrinking? Are there signs of disruption by new market participants, new technologies or new business models, or all of these together?

The market for recorded music and the surrounding music business are a good and a well-known example of how technological innovations have led to immense changes: from shellac through vinyl, tape and cassette to CD and minidisc, right up to MP3 and streaming. With equally immense repercussions on the market participants along the entire value chain: music labels, press plants, manufacturers of playback devices, record shops, and of course, the artists.

Are you now being overcome by a strong impulse to say this?: "But we know what is going down in our markets, we're in there every day!" Don't let yourself be fooled by your reflex to follow your gut instinct. Look at the figures, data, and facts with your management team. For your most important strategic decision of where, when, and how you want to deploy your limited resources, it makes a substantial difference whether you want to move in fast-growing markets with high demand or achieve higher market penetration in saturated markets with existing products. In the first case, you have to pay increased attention to adapting your production capacities and volumes at the right time in reaction to rising demand. In the second case, you have to assume rising distribution and marketing costs.

Even if extrapolating from the past to the present and into the future must be treated with caution, insights on market development up to now can provide viable indications for future market dynamics.

DETERMINE MARKET POTENTIAL

Just imagine that you want to sell on the German market jeans for adults that were manufactured abroad. How large is the market potential? Let us do a quick "back-of-the-envelope" calculation. The total population in Germany is around 83 million. Let us assume that your envisaged target group are "adults" in the 40 to 59 age group. That is approximately 24 million people (Statista (2022)) – or 24 million potential buyers. If every person in this target group buys on average two pairs of jeans every year, that translates into potentially around 48 million pairs of jeans for this age group. In 2021, 110 million pairs of jeans were sold in Germany across all age groups. With approximately a 28 percent share of the total population, this means that about 31 million pairs of jeans were sold in your target segment. So, the purchasing frequency therefore averaged about 1.5 pairs of jeans per year. Let us make a conservative assumption for this age group with its high purchasing power and take an average sales price of €100 for each pair of jeans, this comes to a segment turnover of €3.1 billion. That is a ballpark figure.

For calculating market potential, there is a simple formula:

Winning formula

MARKET POTENTIAL = TARGET GROUP SIZE × PURCHASE FREQUENCY × VOLUME PER BUYER × PRICE

One challenge in this calculation is estimating the influencing factors that could strongly affect market potential, for example, product life cycle.

How far back should your retrospective go? As a general rule, five years are a good time frame for recognizing changes and their causes.

STORIES FROM THE FIELD

The following story from a consultancy project illustrates how important it is to know the real market potential.

In the business unit of a globally operating med-tech company, there was a regional market in Eastern Europe that exceeded all the other markets in the business unit in all product segments. For this reason, it was included in the random sampling of markets to investigate market potential.

After we had recorded the number of relevant clinics in this Eastern European market using external data and superimposed these on the clinics mapped in the customer relationship management (CRM) system, we discovered that not even 50 percent of the existing clinics were recorded in the CRM system. Despite having a large sales team when compared to all the other markets, less than 50 percent of market potential was being addressed. That meant that the market was being worked far too little and the real market share was in fact far behind previous estimates. This result prompted the company's management to make an immense hike in the sales team in this market, and after farther reaching analysis, in other markets as well. Reinforcing the sales team thus led to a significant increase in sales.

MARKET

Which markets and market segment are most relevant for you? Get yourself an overview of the existing and possible potential. You will be surprised at what you discover about your own playing field when you dare to come out from behind your "organizational blindness", so to speak, and take the outside perspective. Maybe you will discover a profitable niche, understand the logic of market dynamics better, or, now that your organizational blindness has been "cured", recognize which opportunities are still available.

KEY QUESTIONS:

1. Which markets are we active in today?

2. How are our relevant markets developing?

3. What market potential do our current markets offer?

4. What time and resources will we have to put in to leverage the existing market potential?

5. Where are attractive future markets already today or where are they emerging?

COLLECT DATA

Potential sources for gathering data are, for example:

- Government Statistical Offices (for example, US Census Bureau, EU Eurostat, German Federal Statistical Office)
- Chambers of industry and commerce
- Industry associations
- Market studies (for example, by market research institutes or consultancy firms)
- Own market research

We recommend that you compile your own market analyses, irrespective of whether they are based on expert discussions or customer surveys, if no informative market data or studies are available.

TIP

In an era of "big data", the creators of market analyses often lose themselves in the details, so devise a systematic approach before you start. Which data is important to make inferences about the relevant market? Where will we find this data? It is not a question of analyzing the entire market. Instead, the objective is to get reliable facts and figures to check the plausibility of your assumptions and perceptions of market activity.

ANALYZE THE DATA

Look at every market and every market segment individually. Make a point of varying your analyses according to region. This will ensure you do not stay locked into any internal logic the business units might have. Proceed in three steps:

1. Examine the size of the market.
2. Assess how the market is developing.
3. Calculate your market potential.

CAUTION

Don't be afraid of incomplete data! It is not always possible to find all relevant information. Approximate as best you can – it is better to have "fuzzy" data than none at all! You will get further by knowing that there will be inaccuracies in the knowledge than by not having a market analysis at all.

SOURCES

ANALYSIS

MARKET CAPACITY _____

MARKET POTENTIAL _____

MARKET VOLUME _____

MARKET SHARE _____

QUALITATIVE OBSERVATIONS

FORMULATE INSIGHTS

INSTRUCTIONS

Once you have compiled the data you need, it is also important to describe the data in text form so that you can interpret them and derive insights immediately. In this process, you should focus less on individual figures but more on the direction the market is moving in, and the opportunities and challenges associated with this development.

EXAMPLES

- Europe: saturated market for product segment XYZ.
- Substantial growth of +10 percent CAGR can be expected up to 2030 in all regions, customer segments and products.
- High market potential can be identified in APAC, especially EUR X million for market innovation X.

COMPETITION

HOLD YOUR OWN AGAINST THE COMPETITION

"Competition is a process for separating the slackers from the industrious."
Hermann Simon, German management consultant and entrepreneur, originator of the Hidden Champions idea

"Who are your competitors really?" The answers to this question could either amuse or shock you: From "We have no competitors!" to up to 10 different nominations from five interviewees from the management team, you will get everything. But your ignorance or arrogance will not stop your customers from buying from someone else.

Direct and indirect competition

What alternatives do customers have to your offerings? There are direct and indirect alternatives. British budget airline Ryanair is in direct competition with airlines like easyJet, which operate in the same segment and on the same routes. However, these providers also compete indirectly with offerings from rail and bus companies (like Flixbus in Germany), or customers' ability to go by car. In the wake of covid-19, airlines with relevant offerings for business travelers are now increasingly competing with new market participants, providers of SaaS video conferences like Zoom. Their offerings have made a large portion of business trips obsolete and have therefore substantially changed the rules of the game in the market for business trips.

Customer requirements are decisive in determining which game you can play. They delineate your playing field with its segments. The competitors are the opposition that wants to prevent you from scoring goals with your customers and ultimately tries to score more goals than you itself. What is the right positioning for your company to succeed and leave the field victorious?

BEATING THE COMPETITION

Michael E. Porter (1980) examined and named the most recognized strategies for companies in competition. He identified three generic strategies.

1. Cost leadership
2. Differentiation strategy
3. Niche strategy (focus)

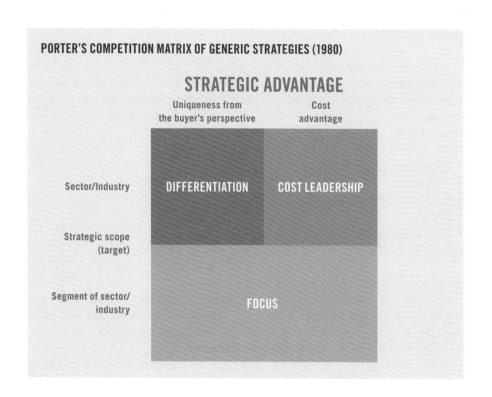

PORTER'S COMPETITION MATRIX OF GENERIC STRATEGIES (1980)

STRATEGIC ADVANTAGE

	Uniqueness from the buyer's perspective	Cost advantage
Sector/Industry	DIFFERENTIATION	COST LEADERSHIP
Strategic scope (target)		
Segment of sector/industry	FOCUS	

COST LEADERSHIP

Cost leadership means that your company has the lowest costs in comparison with competitors for creating and marketing a beneficial offering for their customers. With this cost advantage, you can even still emerge victorious in the end from a price war. While the competition slides into the red, you are still making profits. Cost leadership results from an organization that is optimized for efficiency by exploiting economies of scale, scope and experience. Economies of scale arise when your unit costs fall as your company size or volume of production increases. Economies of scope emerge when you can spread fixed costs across several products and thus achieve lower unit costs per product. Economies of learning, or experience curve economies, are evident in your productivity: With the same cost level, you can produce more than you previously did. Cost leadership does not automatically mean price leadership. It is your choice whether you utilize your cost advantages for a low-price policy or if you want to use the cost savings to invest in achieving a qualitative differentiation for your products. However, if you want to be a price leader, then cost leadership is the crucial prerequisite.

JUST BE DIFFERENT

What you can do better or where you differ from your competitors can make a difference to your customers – if they perceive this difference positively. Appreciated differentiation creates a product area with a certain amount of scope for price setting and customer loyalty. Key methods of differentiation are (cf. Mintzberg et al., 1995):

- Price leadership
- Image/brand
- Service/Customer support
- Design
- Quality leadership
- Undifferentiated versus non-differentiated offerings

Anyone who wants to be a price leader in a low-price segment has to be a cost leader, otherwise a more reasonably priced competitor can always undercut them. If you aim for cost leadership, you need high production and sales volumes to exploit economies of scale, scope or productivity. For this reason, you have to address the mass market. Instead of using cost benefits for rock-bottom-price leadership, you can use them to increase other elements of customer benefit (for example, brand, after-sales service) and achieve a higher price. If you want to be the highest-price leader in the high-price segment, you have to be a quality leader. Producers of premium or luxury products must have mastered the entire spectrum of product attributes like design, function, branding and image.

IN THE NICHE

Niches can be very profitable, as Hermann Simon (2007) showed with the Hidden Champions among German SMEs. Anyone who concentrates on specific customer groups, products or geographic markets can create offerings that cover customer requirements in those niches more suitably and cost-effectively than the offerings of competitors focused on the overall market.

TAKE DIFFERENT PATHS

Should you follow several strategies in parallel? No! According to Porter, this will not bring success, as the strategies contradict each other in their internal logic. How do you think you can become a cost leader if you are banking on innovations at the same time and have to fork over a lot of money for research and development? But to every rule, there is an exception! Hybrid competitive strategies attempt to combine cost leadership and differentiation (see for example, Michael Dell's original business model), whether simultaneously, sequentially (see for example, Toyota with the introduction of the Lexus premium brand) or multi-locally. In emerging countries, international technology companies often offer their high-quality products in low(er)-tech versions which are also produced locally and thus more cost-effectively (see for example, General Electric's portable ECG for the Indian market). Hybrid strategies require a well-designed brand strategy.

Kim und Mauborgne (2004) proposed a further option with their "blue ocean" strategy. The idea is to change the strategic competitive environment and make competition irrelevant through value innovation. Customers' key value criteria when buying a product (price, convenience, design, etc.) are determined by market analyses and their fulfilment evaluated and visualized (value curve) for existing competing offerings. To create a "blue ocean" product, it must then be examined which benefits can be reduced or eliminated in comparison to the existing offerings and which should be developed or newly added.

RED OCEAN STRATEGY	BLUE OCEAN STRATEGY
Competition in existing market	Creation of new markets
Beat the competition	Avoid the competition
Use existing demand	Develop new demand
Direct connection between value, price and costs	Eliminate the direct connection between value, price and costs
Orient the entire system of corporate activity towards strategic decisions on differentiation or low costs	Orient the entire system of corporate activity towards differentiation and low costs

The concept of value innovation calls Porter's classic competitive strategies into question, according to which successful companies outside of niche markets are either cost leaders or quality leaders. Using a blue ocean strategy, you leave the bloody "red ocean", the saturated market with stiff "value-for-money" competition, overfilled with fellow competitors all offering interchangeable products.

Before you choose this path, you should first check whether your company really is swimming in the red ocean and needs a blue ocean strategy for its survival. Because these oases of bliss are not easy to find, the road there is often onerous and at the end of the road, the oasis could turn out to be a mirage.

COMPETITION

Get an overview of the situation: Who are your competitors, how profitable are they compared to you, how do you stand among the competition, today, what structures do your markets have, how do market participants behave, and what market results can be expected?

The competitive environment and its consequences can be investigated with a simple analytical framework. According to the "structure-conduct-performance" model, company and market results (profits, prices) follow on from the behavior of market participants on imperfect markets. Market behavior is expressed in the type and intensity of competition and is mirrored in the strategies and tactics of market participants. Market behavior is predominantly determined by market structure. It reflects the number and size of market participants, the degree of differentiation among offerings as well as the presence of market barriers. Feedback effects occur here, meaning that market results affect market behavior and market structure (for example, Bayer's takeover of Monsanto – results-based behavior – directly reduced the number of actual competitors).

KEY QUESTIONS:

1. **Who are our direct competitors at the moment?**

2. **How do they serve the market? How effective are they from a customer perspective compared to us?**

3. **How is our profitability compared to our major competitors? What are the key factors for profit development?**

4. **Who are our indirect competitors, and what unique benefits do they offer?**
   Who are potential competitors? Who poses the greatest danger, and why?

INSTRUCTIONS

1. Analyze your markets using the Structure-Conduct-Performance model.
2. List your current competitors in each market (segment) by name.
3. Classify the competitors in the competition matrix according to the strategy they pursue.
4. Compare your own profitability with that of your top 3, 5 or 10 competitors.

TIP

Competitors you can compare 1:1 with yourself are not always easy to find. Differences in activity-portfolios and in company organization affect profitability. Nonetheless, you should still attempt to form a peer group and compare yourself to the companies in that group. That is what investors do too when they benchmark a sector or a target company. If you can select your peer group, do it – otherwise, others will do it for you.

CAUTION

The task does not merely comprise getting an in-depth overview of your actual and potential competitors and their behavior. It is also important to understand how they create value added for customers and how they make money. Think about your challenge: to offer customers greater value added than your competitors. And although your direct rivals are important: Do not forget indirect competitors and future new challengers.

MAIN COMPETITORS
by market segment

PROFITABILITY
in percent of revenue

COMPETITION MATRIX Strategy analysis

VALUE

OUTPACERS

DIFFERENTIATORS

COST LEADERS

COST

ANALYSIS OF STRUCTURE, CONDUCT, PERFORMANCE by market (segment)

STRUCTURE	• Many providers/buyers • No entry or exit barriers • Same products (identical or minimally differentiated value offerings)	• Many providers/buyers • Low entry & exit barriers • Similar, but perceptibly differentiated value offerings	• Few providers/many buyers • High entry & exit barriers • Commodities or differentiated value offerings	• One large provider/many buyers • Extremely high entry & exit barriers • Unique products
BEHAVIOR	• Price takers	• Scope for price-setting because of value differentiation due to different customer preferences	• Mutual behavior and result interdependencies	• Price maker
PERFORMANCE	• Negligible market shares (< 5 percent per company) • No superior profits • High value-price performance because of low prices due to competition	• Individual market shares < 10 percent • Negligible superior profits • High value-price performance due to consideration of heterogenous customer preferences	• Individual market shares 10 – 90 percent • High superior profits • Value-price performance ratio depends on the type and intensity of competition	• > 90 percent market share • Extremely high superior profits • Value-price performance reduced because of monopolistic price-setting
	PERFECT COMPETITION	MONOPOLISTIC COMPETITION	OLIGOPOLY	MONOPOLY

STRONG COMPETITION ← → NO COMPETITION

COMPETITION

FORMULATE INSIGHTS

INSTRUCTIONS

Describe the structure of the market and the behaviors of the competitors in the market and draw conclusions from the profitability comparison about how you perform against your competitors. Don't whitewash anything, and also show which competitors pose the greatest danger to you.

EXAMPLES

- Our market is dominated by five competitors with a X percent market share.
- Our five main competitors are ...
- These are all positioned in the market with differentiating offerings.
- In contrast to us, our competitors are operating in a growing market with double-digit profits across the board in their results.

TRENDS

KEEP YOUR EYES ON THE FUTURE

"It is not our task to predict the future, but to be well prepared for it."
Pericles, a leading statesman of ancient Athens

Use your power of imagination – a gift that nature equipped us with – and imagine a tiger. Do you need some help with this? Tigers have colorful stripes for camouflage. They can grow to up to 4 meters long. They can weigh up to 685 pounds. Tigers have the biggest canine teeth of all cats (often around 2.5 inches). They have been on Earth for around 2 million years.

How were we able to survive in our habitat in the face of a menace like this? How was this possible? Think about it and look at yourself.

That's right, a certain ability was required: the ability to recognize problems and solve them creatively.

Let's go on a journey into the history of humanity. Our first ancestors emerged around 2.5 million years ago in Africa. At some point, they began using sticks as weapons and tools. The hand axe is the oldest known tool and dates back 1.75 million years. From about 40,000 years BCE, homo sapiens gradually displaced other hominid species. The "wise human" had developed superior abilities and thus advantages in the evolutionary competition. As artifacts and cave drawings show, there was a veritable explosion in creativity with the development of clothing, tools, and weapons, as well as the creation of art.

This example shows: Creativity is in everyone's nature. Using creativity to generate innovations increasingly faster is becoming the decisive factor for success in the 21st century. Innovation waves are becoming increasingly shorter. Today, product life cycles in the technological field are about 6 to 12 months in many cases. You have no time to wait anymore for the muse or your development department to whisper in your ear.

You have to actively and systematically work on innovations so that you can constantly make new value offerings and survive in the competition between companies.

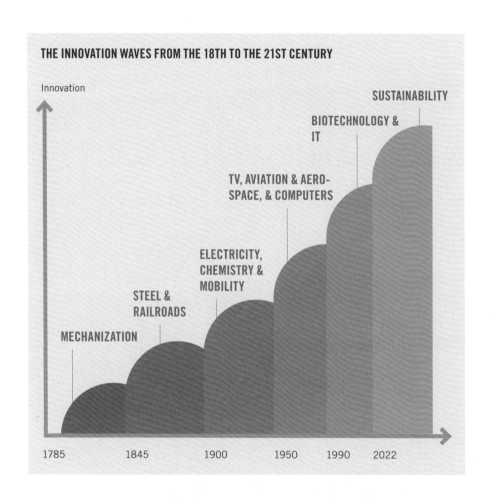

THE INNOVATION WAVES FROM THE 18TH TO THE 21ST CENTURY

Innovation

SUSTAINABILITY

BIOTECHNOLOGY & IT

TV, AVIATION & AERO-SPACE, & COMPUTERS

ELECTRICITY, CHEMISTRY & MOBILITY

STEEL & RAILROADS

MECHANIZATION

1785   1845   1900   1950   1990   2022

In his theory of economic development (1911), Schumpeter demonstrated that a company can temporarily become a monopolist through innovation – until imitators enter the market or the innovation loses its importance because of other developments. Skimming off the temporary monopolistic profits is the economic incentive to innovate. At the same time, it is the invitation to imitators to try and get a slice of the pie for themselves. Schumpeter's competition as an interplay of innovation and imitation leads to the creative destruction of the status quo, or as we say today: to disruption.

Creative destruction = disruption

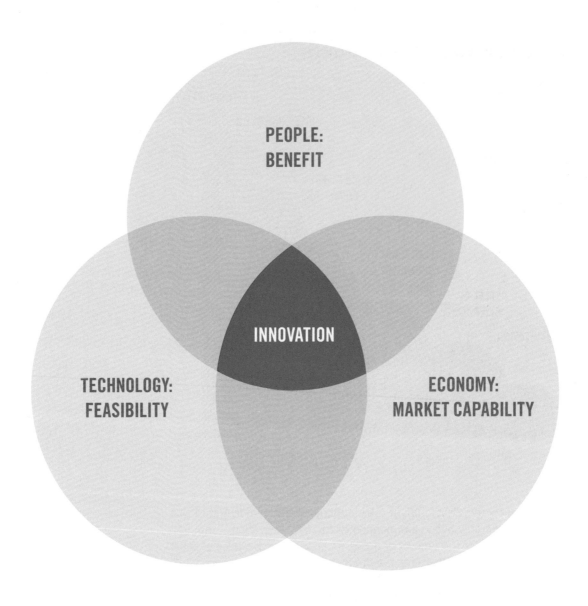

PEOPLE:
BENEFIT

INNOVATION

TECHNOLOGY:
FEASIBILITY

ECONOMY:
MARKET CAPABILITY

Graph: Hasso-Plattner-Institut Academy (2022)

Design thinking as a creative method takes the human perspective as a starting point for developing innovative products, services, or experiences which are not just attractive but also realizable and marketable.

This is certainly an excellent course of action, but how can you shorten this path and identify the trends that affect your company and your business model? Or which trend currents promise innovation opportunities and future potential?

We recommend trend scouting. That means: Get out of your own knowledge silo. View the developments in research, technology, or social culture as well as problem solutions found by other companies (especially start-ups) from a cross-sectoral perspective. This will give you inspiration and targeted stimulus for specific future-oriented fields. Use the leading innovation databases to gain a broad overview of innovations.

Start trend scouting

Build your own "trend radar" with your team to act as an orientation and a decision-making instrument. It will provide an intuitively comprehensible portrayal of the trends that are relevant to you and is the starting point for your strategic innovation work. You will evaluate the trends you identify regarding their relevance for your company, arrange them in the order of their individual degree of maturity on your radar and decide on one of the following action recommendations: act, prepare, observe. When you have a trend radar, you will become sensitized to innovation opportunities at an early stage and can reorient your company strategically on time.

Build a trend radar

Claudia Knacke (2022) drew the same conclusion in the white paper published by trend and innovation consultancy TRENDONE, based on a survey of 85 innovation managers: "Systematic trend management imparts a better sense of orientation to a company – a key competency that enables sustainable growth."

TRENDS

You will find key questions to conduct your own trend analysis here. It is an exploratory process. New questions can emerge from your queries and challenges. Look the truth in the eye to find the proverbial crux of the problem.

KEY QUESTIONS:

1. **Which macrotrends are the most important for the structure of our sector or industry? What are their causes and consequences?**

2. **How are these trends changing the rules of business and the critical success factors?**

3. **What threats do these trends constitute for our profitability and our business model? What opportunities do they open up?**

COLLECT DATA

Start trend scouting by identifying the macrotrends that are relevant to your sector or industry by looking at the major megatrends (for example, climate change). Many of the professional providers of trend analyses initially identify microtrends as inspiration, then cluster these into macrotrends and combine them into megatrends to organize and structure the trend topics. If you don't need completely independent scouting for your specific requirements but just wish to work with general sector assessments, you can utilize the macrotrends that have already been identified in innovation databases.

ANALYZE

Collect the macrotrends in the designated table.
Evaluate them according to:

1. Effect:

How strong do you estimate the effect of the trend on your company?
Scale: 1 = very high to 6 = very low
You will use the "effect" criterion to evaluate the strength of the effect that the trend will likely have. Note that trends can affect individual or several levels of a company.

2. Time of mainstream adoption

When is the trend anticipated within your sector by most market participants?
Scale: 1 = 0–2 years
            to 6 = 10+ years up
You are looking for the time when the "early majority" will adopt the trend.

3. Competence:

How well is your company prepared for the trend?
Scale: 1 = very well to 6 = very little
You will use the "competence" criterion to evaluate how mature your company's reaction to this trend is already today in terms of structures, strategies, projects, or prototypes.

CATEGORIZE

Total up the scores for each section. Depending on the overall points you achieve, the trends can now be categorized into three different stages of action in each circle. Using the innovation categories, you can select the appropriate category field where the innovation in question is occurring.

Watch: 13 to 18 points
The trend is well known. Its influence and speed of adoption among the mainstream is currently still assessed as low. However, the trend should be systematically observed to see how it develops going forward and periodically reassessed.

Think: 7 to 12 points
This trend will have a high to very high impact in the foreseeable future. The trend's subordinate features and the paths of influence should now be understood in detail to prepare specific measures.

Act: 3 to 6 points
These trends have a high to very high impact.

DISCOVERING AND EVALUATING A TREND

MACROTRENDS	CATEGORY	EFFECT	TIME	COMPETENCE
e.g., cybersecurity	Product, service, process business model innovation	1–6	1–6	1–6

TREND RADAR as defined by TRENDONE (2022)

PRODUCT

SERVICE

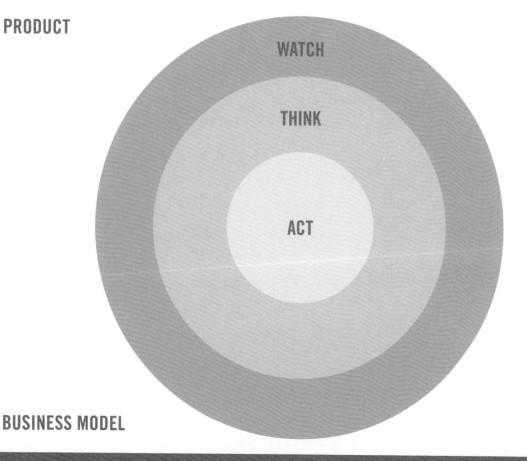

WATCH

THINK

ACT

BUSINESS MODEL

PROCESS

FORMULATE INSIGHTS

INSTRUCTIONS

Formulate the key insights from the categorization of the trends with relevance to your company.

EXAMPLES

- The need for automation will continue to rise and will dramatically change our business model.
- The urbanization of the population is continuing to increase rapidly and is leading to increasingly complex demands on our customers.

BROADER ENVIRONMENT

BRAVE NEW WORLD

"Who will have the greatest effect on digitalization – the CEO, the CTO, the CIO, or Covid-19?"
Social media joke

Whether Covid 19, financial crisis, inflation, supply chain problems, the Ukraine-Russia war, or a shortage of almost all key resources like personnel, raw materials, etc. – one thing is abundantly clear: nothing is as clear anymore as it had previously appeared to be. For many people, that is confirmation that we are living in a VUCA world. The acronym was coined by the United States War College in the era after the Cold War and characterizes our time as increasingly **v**olatile, **u**ncertain, **c**omplex, and **a**mbiguous.

But how are you, your team and your company dealing with constantly changing scenarios? What effects can be expected, and what are you prepared for, and how?

A WORLD WE DON'T UNDERSTAND

A journey to Delphi, the writings or Nostradamus, or looking into a crystal ball is hardly likely to provide you with the best possible assessment of the future. In his book *Antifragile* (2012), Nicholas Taleb develops an evolutionary theory of hazard in which he divides the universe into two types of system: (1) fragile, unstable, and prone to disruption, which will disappear very soon, as well as (2) "variability-loving" systems with a type of hyper-robustness which he named "antifragility". His motto: "Embrace hazard! Affirm chaos!" They are not just disruptions but in fact the true drivers of change. And that is why it is not about trying to predict or understand the future. On the contrary: Even attempting to do so is the road to perdition. It is about the sensitivity, the susceptibility to disruption – and the dilemma that major, unexpected occurrences cause unsolvable problems.

Concentrate on the major influencing factors in the broader environment and derive the scenarios relevant to you. This is how you can focus your strategy and prepare your company for the unforeseeable. The aim is to understand universal trends that go beyond the factors specific to your sector. What is happening around you in the political, economic, sociocultural, ecological, or legal sphere, and how is it impacting on your sector or directly on your business or company?

Antifragility

MAKE YOUR COMPANY CRISIS-PROOF

Identify the major influencing factors in your broader environment. Concentrate primarily on assessing the impact of changes in these factors and not on how likely these changes are. Which changes would be hazardous for your company? Which changes would make your company stronger? Derive the level of resilience of your company in the event that these changes occur. Is your company's resistance fragile, robust, resilient, or antifragile?

The aim is to conduct an educated risk-return assessment. Which changes entail low earnings potential but high risks of losses (not just financial)? Conversely, which entail high earnings potential combined with low risks or losses? You should be very well prepared for the first risk-return scenario or eliminate it by taking appropriate measures. According to Taleb, everything that is fragile will break anyway. To ensure your company's well-being, you do not have to be able to predict the future. Instead, you must remove those things from your future which are fragile and susceptible to disruption. You must therefore make decisions which concentrate on the consequences that you know instead of on probabilities that you cannot know.

BROADER ENVIRONMENT

If you want to attain the best possible overview of the developments in your broader environment, it helps to identify the key factors using a slight modification of a classic in strategic analysis. The P.E.S.(T.)E.L. method is an acronym that stands for political, economic, socio-cultural (technological – excluded here because it is in the Trend module already), environmental, and legal. You should evaluate this overview by reviewing the consequences for your company and its resistance. It allows you to make concrete strategic decisions without having to think in scenarios, probabilities, or eventualities.

KEY QUESTIONS:

1. How are developments in various areas of our strategic environment (politics, macro economy, social culture, ecology, and law) affecting us?
2. How resistant is our company and business model to the anticipated consequences?

ANALYZE

1. Identify the decisive influencing factors from the five areas and describe these briefly.
2. Derive the tangible consequences in various hierarchies (time, intensity) of these influencing factors for your company.
3. Draw your company's fragility curve along the graded tangible consequences:
   Fragile = breakable
   Robust/resilient = temporarily resistant or resistant at low intensity
   Antifragile = learning, self-reinforcing
4. You decide which fragility you wish to remove, and how.

TIP

Instead of simply googling through the macroeconomic data jungle, you can draw on the offerings of various think tanks and research platforms like the Economist Intelligence Unit (EIU), analyses conducted by the major banks (for example, DB Research) or the McKinsey Global Institute.

SOURCES

ANALYSIS

Fragile   Robust/Resilient   Antifragile

	INFLUENCING FACTOR	EXPRESSION OF THE SPECIFIC CONSEQUENCES		
POLITICAL				
ECONOMIC				
SOCIO-CULTURAL				
ECOLOGICAL				
LEGAL				

QUALITATIVE OBSERVATIONS

BROADER ENVIRONMENT

FORMULATE INSIGHTS

OWN REALITIES

HOLD UP A MIRROR

"Many people have a sharp eye for the weaknesses of others and impaired vision for their own."
Ernst Ferstl, Austrian teacher and writer

The greatest personal leadership skill is the ability to constantly question yourself and your company. All too often, empirical knowledge and past successes make executives blind in one area or another. People's own egos get in their way. It is natural that we don't all like to talk about our own faults. Furthermore, power and leadership positions are isolating. Consequently, there is often a lack of open and honest feedback. While frequently requested, it is seldom demanded or accepted. So, if you don't have a Till Eulenspiegel (a medieval chapbook protagonist playing jokes on his contemporaries to expose their vices) in your ranks already, it is high time to let someone hold up a mirror to you.

After you have analyzed your company's broader environment, it is now crunch time. Your own business is going to be put under the microscope unsparingly because the potential scope for action for your strategy will only emerge in the combination of environment and your own capabilities. But where should you start? Usually, some things are in a sorry state, but not everything is bad either.

When Till Eulenspiegel played the fool with his roguish tricks he cunningly pretended to be stupid and took every statement of his fellow human beings literally. In doing so, he held up a mirror to his fellow human beings and thus demonstrated their weaknesses and transgressions. Using laughter and schadenfreude, he exposed them publicly to sharp but unspoken criticism and thus revealed the deficits of his time. You do not have to show up all your insights quite so unsparingly, but the analysis within the management team does require brutal honesty.

What are you really earning money from?

There are two key questions that will help uncover the deficits and inefficiencies: What are you really earning your money with today? If you had three wishes, what would you change immediately tomorrow? Anything goes! Does that almost sound like a practical joke to you already? Then tackle the questions immediately and answer them honestly, yourself or alternatively with your team, or even with outsiders.

However, which products and services the company ultimately earns the most with frequently remains a mystery for longer than you might think. Yes, your own organization, your controlling and reporting system are often too complex. But believe in yourself and your team. You will find them – those products that are produced after all for just that one customer and then put in the warehouse because it doesn't seem to work without doing this, and you can always recoup the money somewhere else. That is the service to the product that consumes 80 percent of total work time and is not remunerated. Yes, we all know the things that we don't want to deal with.

Or there is the universally beloved silo mentality held by area heads and entire business or functional areas who keep their cards close to their chest. At the celebration of life for NBA superstar Kobe Bryant, who died in 2020, basketball legend Shaquille O'Neal recounted an argument he had with the hard-headed superstar. Kobe had hardly made any passes to his fellow players in one game, so Shaq called him out on it on behalf of the team: "Kobe, there is no I in team!" and Kobe responded: "No, but there is a M-E in that mother*****."

You may well know superstars like this from among your own ranks, but good cooperation in a team is probably an even greater success factor in a company than on the playing field.

OWN REALITIES

Aside from analyzing your critical key performance figures and sources of profitability, you also have to look and listen closely. Naturally, this is something that management executives find difficult to do in their own shoes. That is why you should consider – as recommended already in the chapter on qualitative exploratory interviews – whether you should call in a fresh set of eyes from outside at this point. Just a few meetings with key internal people can be the magic ingredient that makes the crucial difference. It is important for all participants to have a familiar safe space – no truths expressed by colleagues or employees can be retrospectively misconstrued or negatively attributed to them. Here you will find a list of key questions that will help you examine your company thoroughly. And look the truth in the eye.

KEY QUESTIONS:

1. **What are the five-year trends in our critical key performance figures and what conclusions can we draw from them?**

2. **Where have we been making money, and where not?**

3. **How do we address the offerings with which we make no money?**
   (Questions 2 to 3 require a breakdown of profit by customer, product group, and geographic region).

4. **What are our major strengths that we could turn into competitive advantage?**

5. **What are our weaknesses that are getting in the way of better performance?**

6. **What would we change immediately if we had three wishes?**

ANALYSIS I: PROFIT CONCENTRATION MAP

In the right-hand column, list the most profitable products or product categories in descending order, stating the share they contribute to your profit. Draw a line when you have identified 80 percent of your total profit. Now list the products or product categories that make up the remaining 20 percent of your profit below this line. If this list is long, you should cut it down so that you can concentrate on your profit earners.

TIP

You cannot work with average figures. Average figures do not say anything – on the contrary, they conceal the truth! The way to improve your performance involves improving or removing the poorly performing parts of a company. Then the average goes up. That means that it is essential to break down your key performance figures – so that you can understand where you are making good profits and where you aren't.

ANALYSIS II: STRENGTHS AND WEAKNESSES

Option A: Exploratory interviews

List the insights you have clustered from the interviews in the strengths/weaknesses matrix. Illustrate some of the insights with pithy anonymous quotes from your colleagues.

Option B: Brainwriting

If you do not have any internal capacity for an exploratory survey, you can conduct what is known as a brainwriting session with your management team. To do this, every participant is given a blank sheet of paper and must use it to list the perceived strengths and weaknesses. After a few minutes, everyone passes their sheet of paper to their neighbor. Each recipient may now only add to the strengths or weaknesses of their predecessor, but not delete any. Repeat this process until the sheets get back to the people they started with. Now present the insights to the entire group and conduct an evaluation on the stated strengths and weaknesses. You can then enter the results into the table provided.

QUANTITATIVE ANALYSIS

PROFIT

80%

20%

PRODUCTS/PRODUCT CATEGORIES

STRENGTHS

WEAKNESSES

FORMULATE INSIGHTS

"ANYONE WHO HAS VISIONS SHOULD GO TO A DOCTOR."

Helmut Schmidt, former German Chancellor

FOCUS

NO HALF MEASURES

"A person who chases two rabbits catches neither."
Confucius

All the data for each of the modules in the situation analysis have now been gathered, analyzed and visualized to the necessary extent. You will have gained some initial insights already. Here comes the next workflow step: Focus.

You now have to reach deeper insights and make decisions that will give your company a clear focus. With all the entailing consequences, with no ifs or buts. Michael Porter (1996), the master of business strategy, sums up the necessary:

"The essence of strategy is choosing what not to do."

Deciding what we do not want to do is something we humans often find very difficult, because we do not like to restrict ourselves in advance and because we prefer to leave ourselves more rather than less room to maneuver for reasons of risk aversion. But with limited resources, there is no way around defining the "don'ts" if we want to do those things that make us "unique" and in which we want to excel. So it is, neither "this one or that one" nor "this one and that one", but instead "this one, but not that one". Because that one, for example, is not part of our DNA or it contradicts our self-perception. We cannot be a "jack-of-all-trades". We must choose.

The Netflix documentary series *Jiro dreams of sushi* brings this home to us very convincingly. The documentary profiles 85-year-old sushi chef Jiro Ono. At some stage, he had decided to run a sushi restaurant with only 10 seats in a Tokyo subway station. We are witnesses to how he created something really big on a very small scale through self-sacrificing dedication and concentration on attaining mastery in his highly specialized area: US$ 300 per plate, 3 Michelin stars and a legend among gourmets. As Japanese author Tanizaki Jun'ichirō said: "[it is] in the mastery … the patina that develops through long years of tireless polishing." Maybe the image of the patina is an inspiration or even a good leit-motiv to attain mastery in focusing your company.

FROM SITUATION ANALYSIS TO TARGET VISION

Strategy workshop I

While you have involved individual colleagues intermittently in planning, gathering and analyzing so far, your entire management team, expanded to include selected initiators if necessary, is now invited to participate in your first group strategy workshop.

The first "to do" is to answer the question, "What is happening in our company, where do we stand today?" It is a fundamental management task to create from the results of a situation analysis a shared understanding among the management team of a company's status quo and from that to develop the target vision for the future strategy. Take your time to discuss the results of the situation analysis in detail as a team. Encourage the participants to question even obvious relationships and look for outliers and anomalies. Questions help. Always. Questions like those that Willie Pietersen, Professor of the Practice of Management at Columbia School of Business and ex-CEO of Lever Foods and Tropicana, likes to ask his listeners in his warm-up:

- Do your products or services have a "winning proposition", a value offering to the customers that creates more value than the offerings of the competition? What do you do better than or different from your rivals?
- Where are you losing against them? Where is your company worse than the competition?
- Which of your products or services are profitable?
- Are your winning propositions also paying propositions?
- Where do you achieve higher profits than the competition?

Discussing the answers to these and further-reaching questions will crystallize the overall answer to "what's going on here", meaning, the factual and true situation. Specifically, that means: What are the causes of the results, what is the background? If you consider your portfolio of offerings, for example: Is it as broad as it is because you want to fulfil every customer wish? Or are you serving customer segments that have developed randomly without careful scrutiny? Get clarity and consensus on the challenges and opportunities in your current arena of playing fields, on potential new playing fiends, on potential courses of action and risks involved as well as on the likely time frames.

Your target vision

Next you have to determine your focus – which playing fields should the company operate on in the future – and define the priorities for the allocation of company resources with the aid of objectives and key results. The results of this process show which strategic decisions (e.g., investments) you need to make, and which operational or tactical measures have to be taken to accomplish your focus. No matter what meaningful strategy you preliminarily derive: Ensure that it is consistent with your idea of the impact that your company wishes to generate in the world. This global assessment will then yield your target vision: "Where do we want to go?"

STRATEGY WORKSHOP I

"Our strategy workshop that time in Dusseldorf with the StrategyFrame® and Mr Underwood and Professor Weigand was a real turning point for our company."
Hans-Jürgen von Glasenapp, Managing Director, BILSTER BERG Drive Resort

Make the first strategy workshop in the StrategyFrame® workflow something special for you and your team. Something that the participants will still want to remember positively even in three years' time. Create the best possible conditions for an intense confrontation with the realities in your environment and of your company. Engage in intensive discussions with your team about your company's starting position and use them to develop new ideas for its future direction. There will certainly be a few differences of opinion. That is part of the process, as long as no personal animosities come to the fore. With this workshop, you are also laying the foundation for a new strategy routine.

When you prepare your workshop, you should clarify the following points:

Key questions

#1: Objective
#2: Duration and dramaturgy
#3: Participants
#4: Meeting venue
#5: Moderation

#1: WHAT IS THE OBJECTIVE OF THE STRATEGY WORKSHOP?

At the end of the workshop, you and your team should have developed a shared target vision for the future based on the situation analysis. The objective is not to elaborate the entire strategy in detail. On the contrary, if you want to achieve too much at once, you will be disappointed. Generally, not all participants have the same level of knowledge from the outset because they may have only been involved in individual elements of the situation analysis. You must therefore bring the participants "up to speed", to:

- enable a joint assessment of the initial situation,
- understand the challenges and opportunities and
- start agreeing on strategic options.

#2: HOW LONG SHOULD THE STRATEGY WORKSHOP TAKE? WHAT SHOULD THE SCHEDULE ENTAIL?

One day will not be enough. Time and again, we have experienced bosses who did not want to "sacrifice" more than one working day. Time is a limited resource, but do not make false economies. Generally, more than a day has passed before all participants have arrived mentally and intellectually and an accepted assessment of the initial situation is reached.

Ideally, you should plan for 2.5 days for the first workshop after the situation analysis. The half day is reserved for the afternoon after arrival at the meeting venue. You can use it to introduce the agenda of the workshop and present the core results of the situation analysis. A dinner with all participants closes the day. Then you can get started straight away the next morning without having to wait for colleagues who are still stuck in traffic. We estimate you will need the next day and a half to reach a shared understanding of the initial situation, evaluate risks and opportunities, and develop potential solutions. The remaining half-day should be used for drafting a target vision and for planning the next steps.

Two-and-a-half days

Are any further team activities required above and beyond the assignment, or inspiring guest speakers who have scaled the highest mountains or executed an Iron Man challenge? Here, too, less is more. Your objective is clear. The workshop should deliver concrete results for the process going forward. That is why we do not recommend any further activities beyond those mentioned here. We also advise against guest speakers who do not contribute anything that is directly relevant to your strategy development or will not play a significant role in your strategy process.

#3: WHO SHOULD PARTICIPATE IN THE STRATEGY WORKSHOP?

Needless to say, the senior management team should take part in the workshop because these executives will be responsible for implementing the developed strategy in all areas of the company. Therefore, early involvement is vital. Of course, you can expand the circle to include other people to gain additional perspectives and inspiration.

But remember: From 10 to 12 people upwards, the complexity of communication and coordination increases significantly. You will have to increase your activation efforts to prevent individual participants from sitting back and switching off or even disconnecting. In addition, every participant who does not belong to the management team alters the team dynamics – that can have a positive or a negative effect. In this case, you should consider additional teambuilding measures to ensure acceptance and coherence in the workshop.

Senior management team

#4: WHERE WILL THE STRATEGY WORKSHOP BE HELD?

After a long period of pandemic conditions, workshops with in-person attendance are highly popular again. Rightly so. Discussions proceed much more dynamically without mute/unmute, sensitivities and emotions are much easier to read, and the coffee breaks can fulfil their important role as catalysts again. However, that does not mean that digital is no longer possible. We designed many successful fully-digital formats in the pandemic years. Naturally, the time and effort for preparation as well as the costs of a digital "hook-up" are significantly lower than a strategy workshop in the countryside with overnight stay, catering, and so on. But be sure to avoid hybrid workshops in which only some of the participants attend in person, while the others join online. This balancing act either works badly, or not at all. Your strategy workshop deteriorates in terms of spontaneity, dynamism, and productivity.

When it comes to the physical venue, you should ensure you choose a pleasant environment with an inspirational atmosphere. The typical business hotels in major cities have suitable conference room facilities. However, we have seldom felt inspiration in such places. Unusual locations far removed from the classic business hotel scene can stimulate reflection. When selecting your conference room in the selected venue, you should avoid rooms with large, unmovable tables and unwieldy seating. You only need a room that is a basic, practical square box – and therefore has enough space to be furnished flexibly and is equipped with adequate and functioning whiteboards and digital presentation surfaces.

Avoid hybrid formats

PLAN ∘∘→   ANALYZE ←↕→   FOCUS ✸   ADAPT ⬡

#5: WHO WILL BE MODERATING THE STRATEGY WORKSHOP?

The workshop moderator can be someone from among your own ranks or someone external. It should be a personality who will be noticed and accepted for both their demeanor and their communication because as moderator they have to simultaneously motivate, provoke, and objectify without letting the workshop participants "steal the show". Do you have a personality like this in your ranks? If you do, then make sure that this person has a résumé and sufficient experience within the company to be acceptable to the participants, is not professionally blinkered and is a generalist rather than a specialist. With the StrategyFrame® for support, this person should then be able to lead the workshop.

Alternatively, you could bring in someone from the outside. This has the advantage of impartiality and neutrality. An external moderator can address and verbalize things – the "elephant in the room" – that could be difficult for an internal moderator to do. Of course, in this scenario too, personality and experience are important. We have personalities on our Strategy Makers team who are familiar with the StrategyFrame® and are able to moderate your strategy workshop.

STRATEGY WORKSHOP I

Before you start the workshop, you should be able to answer "Yes" to these three questions:

- [ ] Have you completed the situation analysis?
- [ ] Have you invited all the participants to the workshop?
- [ ] Were all workshop participants involved in the situation analysis (interview, module processing, etc.)? Or did you share the key questions from the individual modules in the situation analysis with them?

Now you can jump into the detailed planning of the workshop with the following key questions and draw up an agenda:

KEY QUESTIONS:

1. What is the objective of the strategy workshop?
2. How long should the strategy workshop take and what should the schedule entail?
3. Who should participate in the strategy workshop?
4. Where will the strategy workshop be held?
5. Who will be moderating the strategy workshop?

KEY FIGURES:

For 1. OBJECTIVE:

_____

_____

_____

For 2. DURATION:

_____

For 3. PARTICIPANTS:

_____

_____

_____

_____

_____

For 4. VENUE/ROOM:

_____

For 5. MODERATION:

_____

_____

_____

_____

_____

DAY ___.___._____

TIME	MODULE	FORMAT	EQUIPMENT	WHO	WHERE	RECOMMENDATION
___:___	Arrival and check-in					
___:___	Welcome address					30 mins.
___:___	**Check-in:** What are your expectations for the workshop and the strategy process?					30 mins.
___:___	**Outlook:** Workshop	Presentation				15 mins.
___:___	**Situation analysis I:** Presentation of the results of "Our environment"	Presentation + Q&A				60 mins.
___:___	Coffee break					30 mins.
___:___	**Situation analysis II:** Presentation of the results of "Own realities"	Presentation + Q&A				60 mins.
___:___	**Check-out:** What surprised you?					15 mins.
___:___	**Alternative:** Team activity					60 mins.

DAY ___.___._____

TIME	MODULE	FORMAT	EQUIPMENT	WHO	WHERE	RECOMMENDATION
___:___	**Check-in:** What was the first thing you thought about this morning?					15 mins.
___:___	**Intro:** Presentation of the goals for the day, agenda, golden rules	Presentation				15 mins.
___:___	**Keynote speech:** Why do we need a strategy that works?	Speech				30 mins.
___:___	**StrategyFrame®:** Introduction	Presentation				15 mins.
___:___	**Situation analysis I:** Our environment – Formulate insights	Group formulation + voting				60 mins.
___:___	Coffee break					30 mins.
___:___	**Situation analysis II:** Own realities – formulate insights	Group formulation + voting				90 mins.
___:___	Lunch break					60 mins.
___:___	**Challenges:** Our strategic options and their risks and opportunities	Group activity				60 mins.
___:___	**StrategyFrame®:** Our target objective – Where do we want to go?	Presentation				30 mins.
___:___	Coffee break					30 mins.
___:___	Formulate impact statement (BHAG)	Group activity				45 mins.
___:___	Wrap-up and check-out: xxx					15 mins.
___:___	Evening event					

DAY ___.___._____

TIME	MODULE	FORMAT	EQUIPMENT	WHO	WHERE	RECOMMENDATION
___:___	Intro					15 mins.
___:___	**Check-in:** When was the last time you did something for the first time?					15 mins.
___:___	**Customer benefit & Superior profit**	Group activity + Plenary discussion				90 mins.
___:___	**Set competitive focus:** Define target markets and customer segments	Group activity + Plenary discussion				60 mins.
___:___	Coffee break					30 mins.
___:___	**Set competitive focus:** Define offering portfolio	Group activity + Plenary discussion				90 mins.
___:___	Lunch					60 mins.
___:___	**Define objectives and ...**	Brainwriting + Group discussion				60 mins.
___:___	**... key results I**	Group activity for each qualitative				60 mins.
___:___	Coffee break					30 mins.
___:___	**... key results II**	Moderated plenary discussion				60 mins.
___:___	Define next steps	Moderated plenary discussion				30 mins.
___:___	**Check-out:** What is your feedback and what will you do differently after today?					30 mins.
___:___	End					
___:___	Departure					

STRATEGY WORKSHOP I

1. PRESENTATION OF THE SITUATION ANALYSIS

Customers

Market

Competition

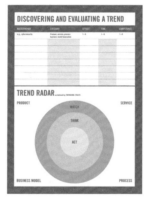

Trends

Broader environment

Own realities

Not all workshop participants were involved to the same extent in conducting and evaluating the situation analysis. For that reason, you must first bring all participants up to speed. Present the results of the situation analysis from the "Environment" (Customers, Market, Competition, Trends, and Broader environment) as well as the "Own realities" modules. Start with providing an "objective" portrayal of the module results without incorporating your own insights and interpretations. This way, you will avoid triggering anchoring effects among the participants. We recommend that you present the quantitative and qualitative results for each module together to create a thematic association. This will make it easier for you to demonstrate deviations or correlations between the forms of analysis and with various topic areas.

LOOK IN THE MIRROR

When you are presenting the results, do not underestimate the emotional reactions of the group or of individual participants. There will be critical queries ("What is the data set employed in this analysis?") or even resistance ("That can't be right. I don't believe that. We'll have to check that again.") or conflicting opinions ("Who said that? I see that totally differently!").

Particularly when it comes to your own realities, emotions regularly tend to run high. When this happens, keep a cool head. Explain the analyses and present their results in their full definition and brutality. That is painful, but absolutely necessary, because otherwise you won't create the notorious "sense of urgency" among the participants to set the process of change in motion. After all, you did not start the strategy process so that everything stays the same in the end and nothing changes. As Einstein famously said: The purest form of insanity is to leave everything as it is and hope something will change."

DIGEST BITTER TRUTHS

For this reason, we recommend that you only present the results on the first half-day of the workshop, without any interpretations or conclusions. Some participants will need a little time to digest the results and assimilate them in a reflection process. Then the participants can discuss them at length during the group dinner or later, in the bar. Some people may find that this continues to reverberate throughout the night and gives them a disturbed sleep. But that is all part and parcel of a successful workshop dramaturgy. In this way, you will avoid hasty emotional reactions the next day when the task is to formulate the insights and develop a shared understanding.

GUIDANCE

1. Attach the module cards from the situation analysis to a pinboard or magnetic whiteboard.
2. Present the results one module at a time.
3. You can always add further information (in paper form for the pinboard or in the digital format you are using). This enables a clear overall picture to develop.
4. Schedule sufficient time after each module for questions.

---

2. FORMULATE A SHARED UNDERSTANDING

CUSTOMERS

· Faccus illuptio. Dae et offict Rit vendebis cus minctem

· Perspel ibuscia dem quid ma iusXimincia quatatem eium eum dellect emosaest

· Quoditat velessunturi ipsunti sin cor sum, coremolent es

Customers

MARKET

· Peroresto est volupta temolupta ipiet qui tem rerum eum adit quam doluptaque molorer

· Stions equissi ncipis sit lam fugit labor renduci

Market

COMPETITION

· Perspel ibuscia dem quid ma iusXimincia quatatem eium eum dellect emosaest

· Quoditat ipsunti sin cores

· Faccus illuptio. Dae et offict Rit vendebis cus minctem

Competition

TRENDS

· Peroresto est volupta temolupta ipiet qui tem rerum eum adit quam doluptaque molorer

· Stions equissi ncipis sit lam fugit labor renduci

Trends

BROADER ENVIRONMENT

· Faccus illuptio. Dae et offict Rit vendebis cus minctem

· Perspel ibuscia dem quid ma iusXimincia quatatem eium eum dellect emosaest

· Quoditat velessunturi ipsunti sin cor sum, coremolent es

Broader environment

OWN REALITIES

· Gitatur si ut omnimenis et eaturio essit que volore dolupta consequi conseque sum etur simos ut laborpossum ducium

· Et fugitate nobicqui cum fugiam in re latus im antum ratiumque cumque voloreseque nobit re ped mo etum quissumquae entesci pitati

Own realities

PLAN ∘◇→   ANALYZE ←◇→   **FOCUS** ✳   ADAPT ◎

"The strategy process is a learning process and a formulation task."
Steffen Bersch, CEO der SSI-Schäfer Gruppe, *HOPE IS NOT A STRATEGY, German podcast #14*

And that is exactly right.

And now it's your turn. Your situation analyis comprises figures, data, facts and statements that have been condensed into results. Now you and your team have to process, understand and interpret these results together and draw conclusions from them. When you are formulating the insights you have agreed on, every single word matters.

INSTRUCTIONS

The way you conduct the formulation process depends on the number of workshop participants:

2 to 4 participants:	Formulate with the entire group
6 to 8 participants:	Formulate in two breakout groups of 3 to 4 participants
9 to 12 participants:	Formulate in three breakout groups of 3 to 4 participants

Proceed module by module. If the participants are split up into breakout groups, each group will work on one module. Use brainwriting as a technique to support the formulation process.

Brainwriting: Each participant individually thinks about the topic and jots down thoughts, observations or suggestions on a notepad or flipchart. You can now use the 6-3-5 method to filter the insights. How does the method work? Each of the six participants writes down three insights and passes them on to the other five participants one after the other. Each participant then adds to their predecessor's insights. You can adjust the 6-3-5 method to the number of your workshop participants.

PROCEDURE

1. Before you start the 6-3-5 rounds, you should clarify the key questions for the module again.
2. Each participant writes down three insights per round on the worksheet. A round should take no more than 5 minutes or end as soon as all participants have listed their three insights.
3. When the round ends, each participant passes their worksheet on to their neighbor (for example, in a clockwise direction). A new round begins now: Each of the participants then adds another three ideas to the worksheet they received. The ideas listed already can be used as inspiration and elaborated, but totally new ideas are also allowed.
4. Repeat step 3, until all participants have written on every worksheet (so if you have six participants, that means after a total of six rounds).
5. Each breakout group then puts the gathered insights on a whiteboard or flipchart. Let each participant select their two most important insights and mark them with sticky dots. Discuss and derive the group's five key insights.
6. The insights of the breakout groups are then presented, discussed and supplemented in a plenary session.
7. Finally, the insights are evaluated again using two sticky dots for each participant and put into a ranking order from this process.
8. The moderator transfers the final results to each module card for the situation analysis.

FORMULATION TIP

Avoid specialized jargon, formulate your insights precisely in a way that everyone can understand. You will find formulation examples on the worksheets for the individual modules in the previous chapter. In the aftermath of the workshop, you can fine-tune the formulations in discussions with all participants.

CHALLENGES

OVERCOME STRATEGIC OBSTACLES

"There is nothing like a challenge to bring out the best in man."
Sir Thomas Sean Connery, Scottish actor

The next task is to understand the implications of the shared insights, identify strategic courses of action and determine their specific challenges.

UNDERSTAND THE IMPLICATIONS

Let us assume that one of the insights you drew from your situation analysis is that the unit profit of one of your products has risen over the past five years although its market share has gradually declined. If you want to understand the implications correctly, you need to understand the concept of cause-and-effect relationships.

For example, competition theory infers a positive relationship between profitability and market share. And indeed, empirical evidence shows that companies with a larger market share are more profitable on average than companies with smaller market shares. Therefore, is the size of market share causal to higher profitability, or are both variables co-determined by other factors? For example, unit profit can rise if you are able to lower unit costs. Market share can decline because new competitors have entered the market (viz. Apple and Samsung's loss of market share because of the expansion of Chinese manufacturer Xiaomi) or because market segments have changed relative to each other because of changes in customer preferences (size of mass market against size of the premium segment). Just consider the fast-growing "affordable luxury" segment for fashion accessories with suppliers like Michael Kors or Coach.

When you discuss the implications, you should proceed just as unsparingly as you did in the situation analysis. Truth and clarity must have top priority because the implications will determine the fate of your company. You should rank the implications according to how they affect the rules of success for your company or your sector, and which risks and opportunities arise from the implications for your company.

IDENTIFY OPTIONS

Starting with the risks and opportunities profile derived from the implications, you can now examine the various strategic courses of action. To do this, you should categorize your insights in our extended product-market matrix (Ansoff, 1957; Kotler et al., 2012). It contains two additional dimensions. "Consolidation" comprises options for stagnating markets and crises. "Growth" looks at options for future markets and/or offerings in the blue-ocean strategy logic (Kim & Mauborgne, 2015). This will give you a broad spectrum of options to work with.

At this point, it is only about an initial categorization of the insights, not about making decisions. The modified product-market matrix contains 15 strategic courses of action on the topics of:

- Growth or consolidation
- Organic or inorganic growth (e. g., acquisitions)
- Geographic concentration or expansion
- Developing new but already existing markets or customer segments
- Offering new products or services in familiar markets
- Identifying future markets or customer segments

STRATEGIC COURSES OF ACTION

	REDUCE OFFERING	EXISTING OFFERING	MODIFIED OFFERING	NEW OFFERING	FUTURE OFFERING
MARKET REDUCTION	**1.** **Retreat:** Reduction of offerings and market presence	**2.** **Product-constant market consolidation:** Offer existing offerings in fewer markets			
EXISTING MARKETS	**3.** **Market-constant product consolidation:** Reduction of offering portfolio in existing markets	**4.** **Market penetration:** Gain additional market share with marketing activities	**5.** **Product modification:** An existing product is modified, the resulting value added induces the existing target group to make a repeat purchase	**6.** **Product development:** Developing a product further can induce established customers to make new purchases	**12.** **Offering identification:** Identification of future offerings for existing and familiar markets
FAMILIAR MARKETS		**7.** **Market expansion:** Existing products are sold to the familiar target group in new geographic markets	**8.** **Limited diversification:** Existing products are adapted to new geographic markets and modified for them	**9.1.** **Partial diversification I:** New products are developed for different requirements of new geographic markets	
NEW CUSTOMER SEGMENTS		**10.** **Market development:** Development of new, e.g., regional markets to increase revenue from existing products	**9.2.** **Partial diversification II:** Products are modified according to new requirements of new customer segments	**11.** **Diversification:** horizontal, vertical, lateral	Future offerings for future markets/target groups
FUTURE MARKETS/ CUSTOMER SEGMENTS		**13.** **Market identification:** Identification of future markets for existing and modified offerings		**14.** **Future diversification:** New future offerings for future markets/target groups	

CONSOLIDATION STRATEGIES

1. RETREAT: REDUCE OFFERINGS + REDUCE MARKETS

Idea: Gradual exit from unprofitable markets or market segments and discontinuation of offerings

Implementation:
- Discontinuation of entire business operations
- Sale of segment offering and market presence to other companies or investors
- Sale of entire business areas

Benefit: You reduce complexity, save resources, and avoid losses. At the same time, you create room to maneuver for the remaining or for new fields of activity. Furthermore, the sale of business units can contribute to stocking up your "war chest" for acquisitions.

Risk: The risk is low, since you know exactly what you will be foregoing tomorrow. However, exiting business areas and markets can incur costs. In some cases, you can also lose the size necessary to be able to exploit cost-cutting economies of scale and economies of scope.

---

2. PRODUCT-CONSTANT MARKET CONSOLIDATION: EXISTING OFFERINGS + REDUCE MARKETS

Idea: Exit from markets, market segments or distribution channels that are not lucrative or not sufficiently well established. Existing offerings are consolidated.

Implementation:
- Sale of regional business unit
- Discontinuation of market presence
- Exit from individual distribution channels
  (e. g., stationary retail in favor of digital platform)
- Exit from certain customer segments
  (e. g., luxury segment in favor of "affordable luxury")

Benefit: You free up resources to be able to concentrate on well developed markets with better potential.

Risk: You lose established market access and leave the field to the competition. If you enter the market again, you will incur entry costs. Then you may potentially have to overcome new market entry barriers and hold your ground against the established competition.

---

3. MARKET-CONSTANT PRODUCT CONSOLIDATION: REDUCE OFFERINGS + EXISTING MARKETS

Idea: You do a targeted clear-out of loss-makers or resource-guzzlers in your offering portfolio.

Implementation:
- Closure or disposal of entire business areas
- Reduction of product segments, product lines or special products in all or selected markets

Benefit: You free up resources for the further development of your core business or alternatively your profit drivers. The costs of your value chain can fall if, for example, you were unable to produce or procure specific product groups locally.

Risk: The risk is low. You can calculate exactly what the exit from the business field or the products will cost and how much revenue will be lost. One thing is probably certain: Your competitors will be pleased.

GROWTH STRATEGIES

4. MARKET PENETRATION: EXISTING OFFERINGS + EXISTING MARKETS

Idea: Try to serve existing markets more intensively with existing offerings.

Implementation:
Greater market penetration by:
- Increasing marketing activities
- Reducing prices
- Acquiring a competitor in the existing market
- Customer loyalty and purchase incentive programs
- Improving sales team competence and/or increasing sales channels and sales resources

Benefit: You create greater demand in the existing market through higher sales to established customers and acquisition of new customers.

Risk: You are familiar with the market, which keeps the risk low, especially if you are in a growing market, whereas in saturated markets your growth potential is clearly discernible. Cost per sale rises significantly with each additional gain in market share. In addition, you have to poach customers from your competitors and your rivals will respond in kind to this.

---

5. PRODUCT MODIFICATION: MODIFIED OFFERINGS + EXISTING MARKETS

Idea: You modify your offerings somewhat. The resulting value added induces the existing target group to make a repeat purchase.

Implementation:
- Modification of packaging, product features, material use, or amounts
- Offerings of special or limited editions

Benefit: You know your target group and offer them new purchase incentives with modifications that are easy to implement. You might also increase purchasing frequency this way.

Risk: The growth potential is in the established customers to whom you are giving new incentives to buy. At the same time, your risk is low because you can test the modifications in small batch numbers to see whether and how well they are accepted.

6. PRODUCT DEVELOPMENT: NEW OFFERINGS + EXISTING MARKETS

Idea: You aim to satisfy established customer requirements in existing markets with new offerings.

Implementation:
- Development of new products or product lines and service offerings
- Substitution of existing offerings with follow-on products
- Development of new brands

Benefit: You will be an innovation leader satisfying existing requirements with new products. This will give you a competitive edge because of unique products or cost benefits.

Risk: You could be left saddled with high development costs because customer acceptance and thus market success are unknowns.

---

7. MARKET EXPANSION: EXISTING OFFERINGS + FAMILIAR MARKETS

Idea: You sell existing products and services to the familiar target group in new geographic markets.

Implementation:
- You enter new geographic markets with your existing offering portfolio.
- You can attempt to acquire an established supplier in the regional market to overcome market entry barriers faster.

Benefit: You use your existing competencies and gradually increase your sales potential by opening up additional potential in other geographic regions.

Risk: Customer requirements and preferences in a different geographic market could deviate tremendously from those in existing markets. You will encounter local competitors that satisfy customer requirements and preferences better than your existing product offerings. Localizing your market strategy will incur additional costs.

8. LIMITED DIVERSIFICATION: MODIFIED OFFERINGS + FAMILIAR MARKETS

Idea: You modify your existing offerings to be able to sell these to your target customers in other geographic markets.

Implementation: Modify your offerings according to regional regulatory, linguistic, cultural, and technical requirements.

Benefit: You utilize existing competencies and resources to position your modified offerings in the target markets and thus increase your sales potential.

Risk: The modifications you make to fulfill the requirements of the target market are cost-intensive and time-consuming (e. g., getting approval for medical products in a new geographic markets) and customer acceptance is an unknown.

9.1. PARTIAL DIVERSIFICATION I: NEW OFFERINGS + FAMILIAR MARKETS

Idea: New products are developed and sold for familiar customer segments in other regional markets.

Implementation:
- Development of innovative offerings that are tailored to specific regional customer requirements
- Development of new brands for an adapted regional targeting and definition of other markets
- Acquisition of a competitor with market access and product innovation in familiar customer segment
- High level of marketing activity
- Development or adaptation of sales structures and distribution channels for the new market

Benefit: You can address specifically attractive regional markets with high potential. In some cases, the regional product innovation can also be used for existing markets.

Risk: If the new offerings are only developed for a regional market, the costs of development and of building a new marketing and sales architecture may not be scalable due to limited demand potential.

9.2. PARTIAL DIVERSIFICATION: MODIFIED OFFERINGS + NEW CUSTOMER SEGMENTS

Idea: Modification of existing offerings according to the requirements of new customer segments.

Implementation:
- You will reach a younger target group with a slightly modified offering (e. g., insurance) through a new sales channel (e. g., e-commerce)
- Adjustment of marketing for the new customer segments
- Development of a special brand appropriate for the target group to address the new customer segment

Benefit: You transpose your modified products onto new customer segments with manageable time and expense and exploit new growth potential without significant market entry barriers.

Risk: A lack of reputation or customer awareness in the new market segment can cause problems. Or the modifications to your product may not sufficiently satisfy the requirements of the new customer segment because you are still lacking specific knowledge of the target group.

---

10. MARKET DEVELOPMENT: EXISTING OFFERINGS + NEW CUSTOMER SEGMENTS

Idea: Increase sales of your existing products by expanding into new markets, market segments or customer segments.

Implementation:
- Invest into developing new market or customer segments
- Invest into tapping new geographic markets

Benefit: If your company has offerings that meet demand in different markets or customer segments, this strategy is the next logical growth step.

Risk: Compared with the market penetration or product development strategies, the market development strategy involves a higher risk. Foreign markets differ significantly in purchasing power and consumer habits. But new customer segments can also spring a few surprises.

11. DIVERSIFICATION: NEW OFFERINGS + NEW CUSTOMER SEGMENTS

Idea: Tap new markets with new offerings.

- **Horizontal development:** You develop new products that are rooted in your company's core business area. You utilize available expertise along your existing value chain. That means there is a material connection between the existing offering and the new offering, even if the new offering solves customer requirements differently (example: a sausage manufacturer also offering vegetarian products).
- **Vertical:** You develop a new offering at an upstream or downstream stage of the value chain (example: an automobile manufacturer acquires a supplier and also offers their products, like for example, tires or accessory components). This enables you to reduce dependencies, secure market shares, and expand your own growth.
- **Lateral/diagonal:** There is no material connection between the old and the new product-market combinations anymore. You might potentially use one of your company's strengths (example: gas station becomes a mini supermarket).

Benefit: Diversification will make your company less dependent on individual products, product groups or business areas. This enables you to compensate for growth problems or market weaknesses in one area with a new area.

Risk: Diversification is meant to spread risk. However, this strategy carries high risks because you are supposed to start operating in new markets with new products. You have to expect high upfront costs for market analyses, product developments, marketing measures, and brand development, as well as the cost of investment in new infrastructures.

FUTURE/DISRUPTIVE STRATEGIES

12. OFFERING IDENTIFICATION: FUTURE OFFERINGS + EXISTING/FAMILIAR MARKETS

Idea: Identification of innovative or disruptive offerings for existing or familiar markets.

Implementation: Utilization of a new operational and/or financial approach (example: fintech startups) to create an offering portfolio that is good enough for the lower mainstream segment according to the prevailing standards of the sector or the market.

Benefit: You address oversupplied customers in the lower segment of the main-stream market with discount prices. You achieve cost advantages and profit margins that are required to win business at the lower end of the market.

Risk: High risk because there is no empirical data available for the new business model or for market acceptance. That is why disruptive business models must be separated from core business.

---

13. MARKET IDENTIFICATION: EXISTING/MODIFIED OFFERINGS + FUTURE MARKETS/CUSTOMER SEGMENTS

Idea: Identify future markets for an existing or modified offering (example: Cirque du Soleil).

Implementation: You reduce the "traditional" attributes of your service in your offering (Cirque du Soleil: no animals) but increase the service by improving retained attributes or by adding new attributes (Cirque du Soleil: world-class acrobatics combined with excellent musical theater) and thus create a better customer experience.

Benefit: You target non-consumers with this: customers who in the past did not have the willingness or capacity to pay to consume the offering.

Risk: The business model must be profitable with low prices per unit sold and with initially small production volumes. Gross margin per unit sold will be markedly lower. Disruptive business models must be separated from core business.

Idea: Identify or create a blue ocean, a market with little or no competition (example: AMAZON's cloud server offering AWS).

Implementation:
- Forge radical new paths
- Redefine the rules of success
- Create an uncontested marketplace with new demand
- Break down the relationship between customer benefit, price, and costs
- Orient your entire system of corporate activities to striving for differentiation and low costs
- Participate in innovative startups or acquire one

Benefit: If you find a combination like this and are a "first mover", you will be operating in a market with great future potential and high profits but little competition.

Risk: You are making a bet on the future. Naturally, that is extremely risky. There are no guarantees whatsoever. Even the best situation analyses won't help here. That is why disruptive business models must be separated from core business.

DETERMINE CHALLENGES

In this phase, it makes sense to name the major challenges for your company. These should be derived clearly from the risks-and-opportunities profiles and the options identified. A strategy and its target vision are seldom completely indeterminate. After all, you are operating in a conflict area between your "own realities" and the realities of your environment.

Generally, there will be several challenges you will have to face with your strategy. Clearly naming these challenges is a call to action and helps set the correct focus for your target vision. Additionally, you will create the sense of urgency that constitutes a vital component of the narrative (storyline) of your strategy.

COMMUNICATION

The insights formulated in the workshop will form the basis for the first component in a coherent line of reasoning to explain your strategy. Ideally, linking up your answers to the following key questions in a coherent way will illustrate both the necessity and urgency for a new strategy and make it comprehensible:

- Why do we have to change?
- Why do we have to act just now?
- Which external factors are forcing us to make conclusive decisions?
- What internal homework do we have to do?
- Where can we build on our strengths?
- Which challenges do we have to concentrate on?

TIP

Review these bullet-point questions and the acquired answers after the workshop for consistency of formulation.

CHALLENGES

Once you completed formulating the insights from the situation analysis during Strategy Workshop I, you and your team must take the next step and clarify the key challenges to master. If the implications, courses of action and their consequences are not clear, there will be no urgency to act, and there will also be no indication of whether you are on the right path to realizing the target vision. You can address the three steps – implications, courses of action, and consequences – in a group discussion. In this way, participants can explain their viewpoints openly as regards the results of the analysis and the insights.

KEY QUESTIONS:

For 1. **RETREAT:** Which markets or offerings are stagnating or losing?

For 2. **PRODUCT-CONSTANT MARKET CONSOLIDATION:** In which markets are your offerings not profitable?

For 3. **MARKET CONSTANT PRODUCT CONSOLIDATION:** Which offerings are not profitable in your markets?

For 4. **MARKET PENETRATION:** Where do you have yet untapped potential?

For 5. **PRODUCT MODIFICATION:** How can a modified offering cover additional requirements or encourage established customers to purchase higher volumes?

For 6. **PRODUCT DEVELOPMENT:** How can your customers' requirements be satisfied in a different way?

For 7. **MARKET EXPANSION:** In which other regions of the world are there similar requirements?

For 8. **LIMITED DIVERSIFICATION:** In which regions of the world are there similar requirements which you can satisfy with modified offerings?

For 9.1. **PARTIAL DIVERSIFICATION:** Which new sectors are lucrative?

For 9.2. **PARTIAL DIVERSIFICATION:** Which target group could you serve profitably by modifying your offerings?

For 10. **MARKET DEVELOPMENT:** Which other target groups can benefit from your offerings?

For 11. **DIVERSIFICATION:** How could requirements develop in three, five or ten years?

For 12. **OFFERING IDENTIFICATION:** Are there new operational or financial approaches for satisfying basic requirements at discount prices?

For 13. **MARKET IDENTIFICATION:** Can you gain current non-customers by offering new product attributes?

For 14. **FUTURE DIVERSIFICATION:** Can you see undeveloped markets where new demand could emerge?

INSTRUCTIONS FOR IMPLICATIONS:

1. List the expected implications for the individual insights from the modules.
2. In each case, describe how these could change the rules of success for your company or the sector.
3. Briefly describe the risks and opportunities.

INSTRUCTIONS FOR COURSES OF ACTION:

1. Reduce your courses of action: Based on the implications, you can now delete courses of action that are definitely out of the question in view of your risks-and-opportunities profile.
2. Create a range of options: Using the opportunities you have identified and working through the key questions, integrate the insights from the modules into individual courses of action.
3. Substantiate the courses of action: Underpin the options, if necessary, with data from the analysis.

IDENTIFY IMPLICATIONS

IMPLICATION	CHANGE IN THE RULES OF SUCCESS	OPPORTUNITY	RISK

COURSES OF ACTION

	REDUCE OFFERING	EXISTING OFFERING	MODIFIED OFFERING	NEW OFFERING	FUTURE OFFERING
MARKET REDUCTION	1. Retreat:	2. Product-constant market consolidation:			
EXISTING MARKETS	3. Market-constant product consolidation:	4. Market penetration:	5. Product modification:	6. Product development:	12. Offer identification:
FAMILIAR MARKETS		7. Market expansion:	8. Limited diversification:	9.1. Partial diversification I:	
NEW CUSTOMER SEGMENTS		10. Market development:	9.2. Partial diversification II:	11. Diversification:	
FUTURE MARKETS/ CUSTOMER SEGMENTS		13. Market identification:		14. Future diversification:	

CHALLENGES

FORMULATE INSIGHTS

STRATEGYFRAME®

COMPANY AREA

SITUATION ANALYSIS

CUSTOMERS

MARKET

COMPETITION

TRENDS

BROADER ENVIRONMENT

OWN REALITIES

CHALLENGE

TARGET VISION

IMPACT STATEMENT

CUSTOMER BENEFIT

TARGET MARKETS

CUSTOMER SEGMENT

OBJECTIVES

ACTION AREAS

STRUCTURES & PROCESSES

PEOPLE

SUPERIOR PROFITS

CULTURE

OFFERINGS

DATA & IT

INNOVATION

PARTNERS

KEY RESULTS

ROADMAP

WHERE WE WANT TO GO

"Only the person who knows where he wants to sail to will set their sail right."
Jürg Meier, Swiss Emeritus Professor, Dept. Of Environmental Sciences, University of Basel

After you have determined "where you stand" and the pitfalls of challenge have been clearly named, the next step is the new target vision for your company: "Where do we want to go?" However, the target vision is multi-layered and does not comprise just one major objective or other like: "we want to become number 1 or number 2 in the market."

What you have to do here is determine the focus for your future actions. In this phase of the workshop, things will usually start to "hot up". After all, the word "focus" is derived from the Latin word for "hearth" or "hotspot". You will have to lead controversial discussions and make difficult decisions because focusing also means, based on the "You can't have it all" principle, having to give up certain activities, markets, or customer segments. For this reason, there will be executives in your ranks who will also regard "No, we won't be doing that anymore in future," as a decision against them personally, their performance or their aspirations. Leaving all rational decision-making aside, what you need here is tact, empathy, and creativity if you want your fellow executives to feel included in the future vision for your company.

DETERMINE THE FOCUS TOGETHER

For the remainder of Strategy Workshop I, you will work through the following four modules with your team:

1. IMPACT STATEMENT (BHAG)

> What lasting effect do you want to achieve with your company?

The impact statement will form the roof of your target building. It expresses which value-adding contribution your company wishes to make to the economy, society and the environment and be profitable in doing so. As a matter of fact, you can also alternatively use an existing mission statement comprising your vision, mission and values.

2. CUSTOMER BENEFIT & SUPERIOR PROFITS (WINNING PROPOSITION)

> How will you achieve a greater or a different benefit than your competition for your customers? How will that enable you to generate higher profits than your competitors?

Customers will purchase and consume a product from your company if the net benefit of your product, meaning the benefit that the customer subjectively perceives minus the price she has to pay for it, is higher than that of rival products. If you create a higher net benefit than the rivals, you have what Willie Pietersen (2001) calls a "winning proposition". But remember: It is the customer, not you, who decides whether there is a differentiation! The differentiating benefit will attract customers but is not sufficient to win them over. In fact, the differentiation from the competition has to also lead to superior profits. Put differently: The difference between revenue and costs must be higher than that of your competitors. Thus the "winning proposition" has to be a "paying proposition" as well. You want to attract and retain those customers who are profitable for your company. Thus, the competition for superior value added has two fronts: customers and costs.

3. TARGET MARKETS, CUSTOMER SEGMENTS, OFFERINGS

> The competitive focus determines the playing field and forms the core of the target vision: Which markets do we want to serve?

Decide which sectors, business fields, and geographic areas you want to be active in.

> Who should your customers be?

Decide which customer segments you want to serve in the selected markets, sectors, and geographic areas.

> Which offerings do you want to have in the market?
> Which offerings will you not have?

Define your offering portfolio. Decide which products and services you would like to offer to which customers. A key factor for your selection is your expectations and assessments of your customers' future requirements.

4. OBJECTIVES & KEY RESULTS

> Which qualitative objectives do you want to realize, which quantitative key results do you want to achieve?

Your target building comprises the most important priorities for implementing your impact statement, differentiating customer benefit and achieving superior profits for your selected competitive focus. These priorities should portray the "critical success factors" that make the biggest difference to company profits. Keep the number of objectives low: three to a maximum of five objectives are enough. The longer the list of objectives, the lower the probability of achieving every one of them.

The "winning proposition" addresses the market and customers. By contrast, objectives and key results have an inward impact. They show the organization on what to concentrate its energy and resources and how it should be mobilized to realize the "winning proposition" and generate the desired impact.

"A GOAL WITHOUT A PLAN IS JUST A WISH."

Antoine de Saint-Exupéry, French author and pilot

IMPACT STATEMENT

MAKE A REAL IMPACT

Who doesn't know them: the boring or interchangeable mission statements on long corporate corridors? The visions there vary in their slogans between market leader and number one. Seemingly strange interpretations of missions and visions for which one thing is already clear at first glance – nothing is clear here. The entire thing is then garnished with a potpourri of values that frequently either make you lose your appetite or simply don't whet it at all. And yes, mission statements are important, and yes, developing good mission statements is an art. That is why they are so rare.

So why is it that many companies nonetheless try to conduct a mission statement process at the same time as the strategy process? After all, we have read and learned: no strategy without a mission statement. The mission statement is both anchor and guiding star, but often enough it deteriorates into a stopgap, and in the end, it is not a silver bullet either. Of course, your strategy should be based on something significant, but one statement has proven to be true in the past 15 years of our practical experience: Better no mission statement than a mind-bogglingly bad one.

Uncouple the mission statement process from the strategy process

So: all or nothing. Either you uncouple the mission statement process from the strategy process and put the first one before the second one with sufficient time in-between, or you need a new alternative.

Your vision statement will show which mountain you want to climb, meaning what you want to achieve and how achieving the goal feels. Then your mission statement will be your Polaris and describe how you want to scale the mountain.

Along with your corporate values and principles, the vision and its mission reflect your company's action philosophy. They should therefore be oriented towards persistence and sustainability. Time frames are hard to designate in our fast-moving and disruptive times. A vision aims at a time frame of 5 to 15 years. The mission acts as an instruction manual for how the company should fulfil the vision, and determines the short-, medium- and long-term objectives. Clarity on your action philosophy will help you and your organization to make strategic decisions in the face of the challenges in constantly changing environments. For external stakeholders too, like for example, customers, banks, investors, or potential employees, clarity about values, principles, vision, and mission can make the decisive difference.

VISION
Where do we want
to be in 5–15 years?

CORPORATE PHILOSOPHY

MISSION
Why do we exist?
What is driving us?

CORPORATE PRINCIPLES
What do we stand for? What are our values?

Adapted from Esch (2021)

STRETCH THE GOAL

Time is short and therefore precious. If you want to generate real momentum with the power to inspire, we recommend a real alternative that will ensure clarity. We know that many roads lead to Rome. This is one way to give your strategy traction.

In practice, the BHAG method – pronounced "be-hag" – devised by Collis and Porras in the mid-1990s has proven itself. BHAG stands for "big hairy audacious goals" – so large, challenging or daring objectives. This is about the incentive, the search for the impact. And when we talk about truly big objectives, you really have to take that literally.

Your BHAG should be inspiring and long-term and thus raise your company up to the next level. BHAGs are enormous tasks that can take 10 to 15 years to implement. They shift the boundaries of what your company achieves and challenge your team to make immense progress. The boundaries between visions and BHAGs are fluid. When they are defined for the first time, BHAGs often appear to be objectives that are almost impossible to achieve. Think of US President John F. Kennedy's announcement in 1961 that the USA would send a person to the moon before the end of the decade. In 1961, an aspiration like this appeared to be more like a dream than a potential future reality. But by formulating this objective, President Kennedy inspired Americans to make the seemingly impossible possible.

ACHIEVE THE IMPOSSIBLE

However, to give the BHAGs a bit more depth, increase their inspirational potential and thus receive a combination of mission and vision with a hefty shot of adrenalin, we gave the target direction for the BHAG the term "impact". This addition is geared to the impact that the company would like to achieve and has high inspirational potential with the right formulation.

Why impact? Impact statements show how you generate a verifiable sustainable difference in people's lives, in the environment (environmental) and in society (societal) with responsible corporate management (governance). This involves your company's ESG contribution. That means the impact statement closes the gap between BHAG and ESG – and thus sustainability in a holistic sense. Documentation of the results of your efforts is also being increasingly expected by financiers and interest groups. Determining what impact you want to achieve with your actions will help you do this.

STORIES FROM THE FIELD

One of the finest examples of BHAG with a big impact comes from automotive manufacturer Volvo:

"By 2020, no one will die in a new Volvo anymore."

Volvo drew the consequence from this that all new cars would be restricted to a speed limit of 180 kph (112 mph). Very resolute and strong.

There are basically four types of BHAG:

1. **TARGET-ORIENTED:**
   Set yourself a clearly defined quantitative or qualitative objective.

   For example:
   "Enable human exploration and settlement of Mars." SpaceX

2. **COMPETITION-ORIENTED:**
   Compete with a common enemy.

   For example:
   "Crush Adidas." Nike

3. **ROLE MODEL:**
   Imitate the characteristics of another successful company that is not one of your direct competitors.

   For example:
   "Harvard of the West" Stanford

4. **INTERNAL TRANSFORMATION:**
   Concentrate internally on your own changes.

   For example:
   "Becoming the best global entertainment distribution service."
   NETFLIX

The target-oriented version is the most suitable for an impact-oriented BHAG.

IMPACT STATEMENT

Formulating a real BHAG with a lasting impact with your team can release unimaginable powers and even enthusiasm. During Strategy Workshop I, formulating the BHAG heralds the development of the shared target vision. For this reason, it makes sense to separate this part more distinctly from the situation analysis as regards the timing or location. Because while structure and analytical skills tend to be required more for the situation analysis, this requires more creative energy and skills.

KEY QUESTIONS:

1. **What is our great passion?**

2. **What can our company be the best in the world at?**

3. **What drives our economic engine?**
   - **Is it profit per customer?**
   - **Profit per subscription?**
   - **What is our "x" in "profit per x"?**

INSTRUCTIONS

How do you create this type of BHAG with impact? Imagine, you have three circles with the above-listed three key questions: At the interface of these three circles you will find your target-oriented BHAG with impact. You can now separate the three circles from each other. To do this, use what is known as the "magic triangle". Create it in the room with three writable or sticky surfaces. In rotation, your workshop participants can now collect the key points for the individual key questions under extreme time pressure. At five-minute intervals, one participant always switches group. This way, you compel the participants to focus on what is most important and curtail endless discussions. You can do the finetuning on the final formulation after the event too.

TIP

You can also combine the formulation of your BHAG methodically with the formulation of your differentiating customer benefit and superior profits. For example, in one or two sentences. To do this, replace the three circles in the "magic triangle" with the three modules of the target vision - impact, customer benefit, and profits – along with their respective key questions.

CHECKLIST:

Is your BHAG ...
1. ... **audacious enough to inspire?**
2. ... **clear and unequivocal so that it is evident when the objective has been achieved?**
3. ... **in accordance with the company's goals and principles?**
4. ... **realizable over a time frame of 10 to 15 years?**

CAUTION

Before you set a goal, you should ensure that it is inspiring. It is ok if its achievement appears to be almost impossible – that is precisely what makes this goal a BHAG. When you are formulating the BHAG, please avoid merely setting revenue, margin, or market share objectives. Purely financial objectives fail to have an impact, do not generate the desired motivational incentive and are only exciting to a few team members. Revenue and profits are outcomes and not an end in themselves. Describe the issue or the problem (relevance) that you want to solve in simple and suitable language for your main target audience. If your goal is mainly qualitative, you should ensure that there is a clear way to measure success.

SOURCES

FORMULATE
Adapted hedgehog concept according to Collins (2001)

WHAT IS OUR
GREAT PASSION?

WHAT CAN OUR COMPANY BE
THE BEST IN THE WORLD AT?

WHAT DRIVES OUR
ECONOMIC ENGINE?

IMPACT STATEMENT

FORMULATE YOUR IMPACT STATEMENT

EXAMPLES OF BHAGS OR VISIONS WITH IMPACT:

Airbnb: Create a world where everyone can belong everywhere.

Evernote: Remember everything.

Feeding America: Ensuring fair access to nutritional food for everyone.

Facebook: Connect the world.

Google: Organize the world's information.

Michael J. Fox Foundation: Find a cure for Parkinson's disease.

Microsoft: A computer on every desk and in every home.

Spotify: Unlock the potential of human creativity.

Tesla: To accelerate the world's transition to sustainable energy.

CUSTOMER BENEFIT & SUPERIOR PROFITS

BETTER, DIFFERENT AND MORE PROFITABLE

"Don't be afraid to give up the good to go for the great."
John D. Rockefeller, US entrepreneur

Once you have a clear picture of what impact you want to generate, you can define your company's "winning proposition" (Pietersen, 2001). It is the answer to the question of what you will do differently or better than your competitors to generate a greater benefit for your target customers and higher profits for your company.

Thus a "winning proposition" has two complementary elements: differentiating customer benefit and superior profits.

DIFFERENTIATING CUSTOMER BENEFIT

In competitive markets, customers always have a choice. Why should customers buy from you and not from the competition? Describe the benefit that customers will receive from you in comparison to the competing alternatives. Formulate this benefit in simple words, but make it concrete.

SUPERIOR PROFITS

Profits are an economic necessity: without profits or profit prospects, there are no investments. And without investments in new products, technologies, and business fields, a company will not be able to survive in the long term. If your company is not capable of generating above-average profits, competitors with higher operational performance and greater financial resources will force you out of the market sooner or later. The difference that you want to achieve with a differentiating customer benefit must pay off and give you a profit advantage. The revenue-increasing differentiating customer benefit is one side of the profit coin, cost efficiency is the other. However, absolute profit is not very informative without putting it into context against use of resources. That is why we look at your company's profitability measured, for example, by the return on sales or the return on capital employed. Whatever else, you must exceed your capital costs (cost of equity and debt capital). You have profit-oriented superiority compared to the competition when your company's profitability exceeds that of your competitors.

To do this, you should be able to answer the following questions:

- Which investments do we have to make to realize a "differentiating customer benefit"?
- How high are the profits we can expect?
- What risks do these profits entail?
- Which business model do we need to produce the beneficial offerings and launch them on the markets?
- How will this business model improve our ability to reduce costs and/or increase revenues?

DIFFERENTIATE WITH LOW COSTS

"Value innovation" is the magic word from the blue ocean universe (Kim & Mauborgne, 2015). Similar to the "winning proposition", value innovation has two features that are relevant to competition: on the one hand, the benefit that is tailored to the target customers, or "personas", on the other hand, low costs. However, your focus should be on alternatives in the value offering for non-customers to enable you to tap new or even better, competition-free markets – blue oceans.

Value innovation

If you now think about Porter's generic strategies, a feeling of unease should be setting in by now. Isn't innovation or quality leadership incompatible with cost leadership? Not necessarily. The art is in banking on offering features that provide new or additional benefits for the customer but incur few additional costs to your company. Conversely, offering features that target customers regard as "nice to have", but superfluous, are reduced or removed completely. Value innovation is not about expensive research projects and development budgets. When you eliminate and reduce offering features, you generally lower costs. However, at the same time, you also reduce the customer benefit emanating from the feature. Although creating and enhancing offering features increases costs, it leads in return to more satisfied or new customer groups. With the aid of Kim & Mauborgne's (2015) "four-actions format", a "value curve" or "strategic contour" can be derived for customers and the right balance found between adding and removing.

- **Create:** Which features should be added which were not part of the market or sector standard up to now?
- **Raise:** Which feature should be significantly more distinct from the standard?
- **Reduce:** Which feature should be significantly less distinct from the standard?
- **Eliminate:** Which feature should be removed although it is part of the market or sector standard?

REDESIGN THE VALUE CURVE

The "strategic contour" of your relevant market will visualize which offering features the competition is concentrating on and which benefits their offerings provide. You can then compare your offerings, identify market-specific differentiating features, and draw up the differentiating feature catalog for your strategic positioning. The value curve refers to a selected competitor or a strategic group of competitors within your sector. If several curves are portrayed for different companies in a schematic representation, what is known as the "strategic contour" emerges. The horizontal axis depicts the decisive offering features along the most important customer requirements. You have already determined these for your customers in the situation analysis. The vertical axis describes the performance level in your market and is portrayed in simplified form on a scale of low to high.

You can rank your company on the value curve. If your company gets a high figure for one factor, this means that it has a better performance compared to the competition (and the opposite). You can refer to the results from the "Customers" and "Competition" models for this. When you are making the assessment, the appraisals of your market experts from marketing and sales are relevant too, of course. Just like you did for your own company, you should rank the competitors or competitor groups you identified in the situation analysis. Look at the following example from the wine sector.

STORIES FROM THE FIELD

The days when good wine was sold exclusively in darkened glass bottles with a cork seal appear to be long gone outside Germany. Countless packaging alternatives have meantime captured the wine markets right around the world and offer the right solution for every need.

The global market for wine cans is estimated to reach US$ 16,088 billion by 2028. In the forecasting period, this market is set to grow by an average of 7.2 percent per year (Data Bridge, 2021). The rising demand for conveniently consumable drinks and individual portions is the main driver of the market growth. It is being propelled by consumers' preference for ready-to-eat and ready-to-drink products because of a busy lifestyle and hectic working hours. Wine in cans is a trend that developed in the USA and spread to Europe. US movie director Francis Ford Coppola was the first to market wine in cans in 2004 and in doing so established an attractive new segment in the wine market. One of the authors of this book, Christian Underwood, launched the brand HOLY GRAPE as the first wine can brand in the German wine market in 2017 with a few wine enthusiast friends. The small portions of generally a maximum of 250 milliliters, with the easy-to-open pull tab that makes all bottle openers superfluous are particularly suitable for people on the move. The can protects the wine from light and oxygen – important factors for its shelf life. Traditional wine connoisseurs have reservations about the can. And that is precisely what appeals to the young target group of 25 to 35-year-old women: hip, young, cool, and casual – always prepared for the next party. One thing is clear: the can is practical. It fits into every woman's purse, can't break, is lighter than glass and easy to portion out. In addition, it is 100 percent recyclable. None of these are classic offering features in the wine sector, as the authors of the blue ocean strategy already demonstrate.

STRATEGIC CONTOUR OF THE WINE SECTOR AND CANNED WINE

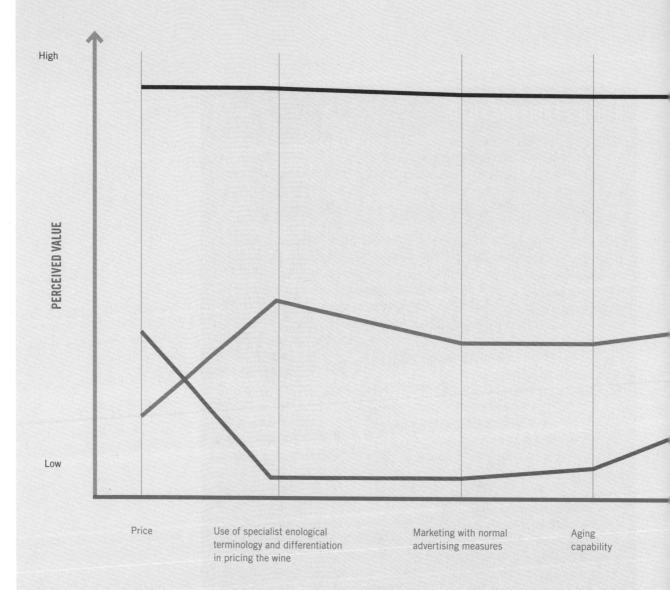

PERCEIVED VALUE

High

Low

Price

Use of specialist enological terminology and differentiation in pricing the wine

Marketing with normal advertising measures

Aging capability

VALUE FEATURES OF THE WINE SECTOR

PLAN   ANALYZE   FOCUS   ADAPT

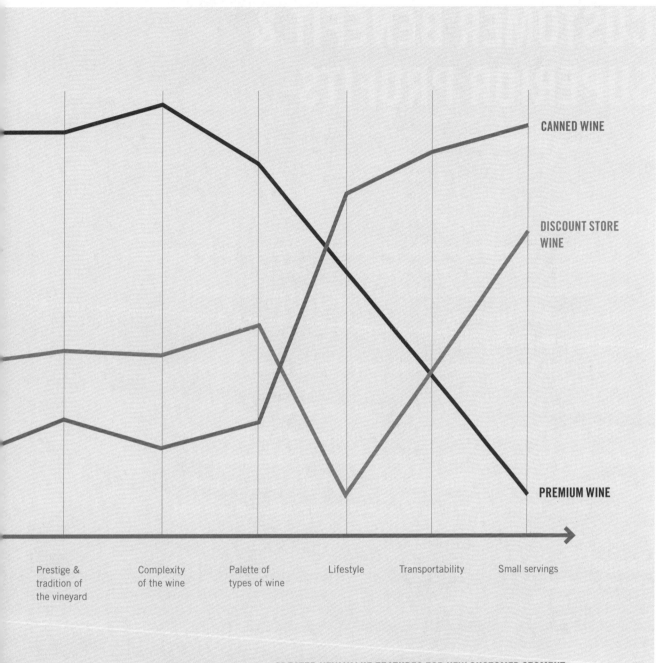

CANNED WINE

DISCOUNT STORE
WINE

PREMIUM WINE

Prestige &
tradition of
the vineyard

Complexity
of the wine

Palette of
types of wine

Lifestyle

Transportability

Small servings

CREATED NEW VALUE FEATURES FOR NEW CUSTOMER SEGMENT

After you have portrayed the current situation, you should now assess the individual offering features along the four dimensions "Create, Enhance, Reduce, and Eliminate". This will enable you to create a new value curve with a "differentiating customer benefit" and lower costs to find profitable demand even in a stiffly contested market with very similar products and achieve "superior profits".

CUSTOMER BENEFIT & SUPERIOR PROFITS

As part of Strategy Workshop I, you should first generate value curves for your company and selected competitors. Then try to redesign your value curve in light of your target vision.

KEY QUESTIONS:

1. What will we do differently or better than our competitors to generate a greater benefit for our target customers and higher profits for our company?

2. What investments must we make to realize the "differentiating customer benefit"?

3. How high are the expected profits?

4. What risks will we run in doing so?

5. Which business model should we introduce, i. e., how will we produce our offerings and bring them to market?

6. Which offering features can we create that did not exist before?

7. Which offering features must we enhance far above the market or sector standard?

8. How will this business model help us reduce costs and/or increase revenues?

9. Which offering features can we reduce far below the market or sector standard?

10. Which offering features can we eliminate that were considered standard up to now?

INSTRUCTIONS:

1. Determine value offerings:
Determine which of your offerings you want to assess in comparison to the competition using a value curve. The products or services should be comparable, meaning that they solve the same problem for an identical customer group. Where there are very heterogeneous customer groups, different strategic contours per customer segment can help.

2. Define offering features:
Write down 5 to 10 highly relevant features of your offerings. Be mindful of the customer requirements you determined and their importance today and in the future.

3. Draw up a current value curve:
Consider each individual offering feature and evaluate its level of benefit as perceived by customers. Draw up the value curves for your major competitors or competitor groups.

4. Develop a desired value curve:
Now define the new value curve for your company's offering with the help of the key questions in the matrix. List the specific features there.

VALUE CURVE adapted from Kim und Mauborgne (2015)

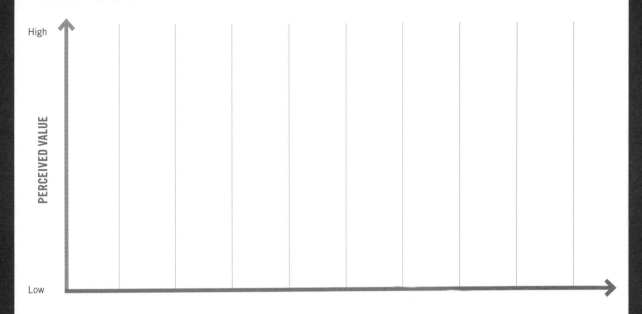

High

PERCEIVED VALUE

Low

VALUE FEATURES CREATED NEW VALUE FEATURES

FOUR-ACTIONS FRAMEWORK

ELIMINATE

RAISE

REDUCE

CREATE

CUSTOMER BENEFIT & SUPERIOR PROFITS

FORMULATE CUSTOMER BENEFIT & SUPERIOR PROFITS

INSTRUCTIONS

Formulating a pithy "winning proposition" has posed a major challenge to many executives in the past.

1. That is why we recommend that you initially list the changes to the offering features descriptively.
2. Then, in a second step, combine these into a single sentence:

"We ... (will make differently or better than the competition) ... in order to generate ... (benefit XYZ) for our (customers) and thus ... (be able to achieve better prices/reduce costs)."

TIP

Do not stick slavishly to the gap statement to work out the "differentiating customer benefit." All you have to do is formulate the benefit in an initial catchy sentence. It is not necessary to put the sentence about your "superior profits" into a formulation that will be accessible to externals. What is important is that all those involved internally know, understand, and support the logic.

EXAMPLES

- Southwest Airlines:
  Operate at lowest industry costs and provide fun-filled air travel which competes with the cost of car travel.
- BILSTER BERG: DRIVING BUSINESS
  We are the preferred partner of the automotive industry for individual automotive fascination. On one of the most demanding racetracks in Europe, with an offroad and dynamic course, we realize individual driving and brand experiences – in a natural setting. That is how we drive our customers' business forward.
- SSI SCHÄFER Gruppe:
  We enable intelligent processes to give our customers better business results. To do this, we offer modular and scalable intralogistics solutions and outstanding project execution. Our innovations and future-proof technologies drive the automation and sustainability of our customers worldwide.

TARGET MARKETS, CUSTOMER SEGMENTS & OFFERINGS

SELECT THE RIGHT PLAYING FIELD

"Once you get on the playing field it's not about whether you're liked or not liked. All that matters is to play at a high level and do whatever it takes to help your team win."
LeBron James, NBA basketball player

Selecting the playing field that matches your company, gaining the best possible fans and offering them an enthralling experience is the core of every corporate strategy. You determine the competitive focus together with your team: In which "target markets" do you want to serve which "customer segments" with which "offering"? That might sound trivial initially. However, from countless discussions about market entry and market exits, lack of focus in customer segments or an overlarge offering portfolio with a thousand items when hardly anyone knows which of them is really bringing in money, our experience shows that it is by no means trivial to find the right competitive focus.

The decisions you make on Day 3 of Strategy Workshop I will have an immense impact on your entire company. Making decisions is not enough. They also must be accepted and implemented. And that too is anything but trivial. But you can make provisions!

DECIDE AND ACT STRATEGICALLY

During the situation analysis, you viewed and sorted your potential strategic courses of action in the "Challenges" module and made initial assessments. Grow or consolidate? Geographic concentration or preferably expansion? Exploit new markets or customer segments? Change your range of products or services? You should have already said goodbye to options with high risk and low growth potential. Now you have an overview of the remaining options in front of you. But how do you now get to the decisions that will largely determine the direction your company should take, and the activities needed to do that? You can now come back to the "differentiating customer benefit". Determine the benefit features for your customers that you want to eliminate, reduce, improve, or create from scratch and transpose your new value offering into your portfolio, customer segment or target market structure.

Across the vertical axis of the product-market matrix, you decide which markets should be exited, retained, expanded (geographically, new customer segments) or approached for the first time because of your "strategic contour" to implement your "winning proposition" and make the "differentiating customer benefit" tangible.

RULES FOR WINNERS

It goes without saying that the decisions about which game you want to play tomorrow on which playing field must be thought through very well, because, after all, you want to win. In their book, *Playing to win,* Lafley and Martini (2013) neatly sum up the rules for winners. We have condensed their insights into "golden rules" for you:

1. Decide explicitly where you want to play and where you don't! Prioritize your decisions.
2. Before you rate a market as structurally unattractive, have a good look to check whether there aren't attractive market pockets for you after all.
3. Pursue no strategy without specific priorities. You can't play all markets and segments – so don't even try.
4. Keep an eye out for possibilities to attack from an unexpected direction.
5. Don't start a war on several fronts. Anticipate the reactions and actions of your competitors so that you have enough strength to still see your decisions through.
6. Check the temptations of potential blue oceans in which seemingly no one is operating yet as to whether you just haven't discovered the "first mover" yet.

TARGET MARKETS, CUSTOMER SEGMENTS & OFFERING

Only you and your team can change your company's game. When you are discussing strategic courses of action with your team, you are discussing the future of your company. Earlier decisions and consequences are in the past, you should treat them as such. If, for example, your current infrastructure is not the right one for the future you envisage, then the investments you made for it are irrelevant. These costs are "sunk" (scuppered), so to speak. They are costs of the past. If you cling on to the past, others will make a plaything of you.

KEY QUESTIONS:

1. Which markets do we want to play in, and which don't we?

2. Which market segments and geographic areas will we serve in the target markets?

3. Which customer segments will we serve within these markets and geographic areas, and which won't we serve?

4. How can customers be segmented usefully?

5. Which products and services will we offer our focus customers, and which won't we offer?

INSTRUCTIONS

We recommend that you conduct the following three steps jointly with the entire group of workshop participants.

1. **Derive impacts:** Use the table with the changed benefit features from the previous model and discuss the impacts on your current offering, on customer segments and markets.

2. **Assess potential:** In the second step, assess with your team the revenue growth and/or cost savings potential on a scale of 0 to 3.

   0 = no potential

   1 = below-average potential

   2 = average potential

   3 = above-average potential

3. **Assess the risk:** Assess the risk according to the potential level of loss as well as the probability that the loss will occur.

   Level of loss = very low, low, moderate, high, very high

   High Probability = impossible, unlikely, possible, likely, very likely

4. **Select course of action:** Mark the courses of action in the product-market matrix for which the potential is at least "2", the level of loss is not assessed to be "high" or "very high" and at the same time the probability of occurrence is not "likely" or "very likely".

5. **Discuss and select options:** Discuss the remaining options once again individually and in detail.

6. **Make decisions:** After the discussion, make clear decisions and don't put them off. Vote on the options. When you vote, each vote in the room counts for the same, and the participants have one vote each for every course of action for one of the following activities:
   • Watch (W)
   • Examine (E)
   • Do (D)

7. **Formulate target markets, customer segments, offerings:** Your decisions, particularly in the "do" column, have an impact on your playing fields. For that reason, be sure to write them down directly onto the module card for all to see.

Make a list of your target markets with the respective customer segments and the relevant offering portfolio. This is about the fundamental structure that you want to enter the playing field with. This structure should be easily comprehensible to everyone, both internal and external. To help you do this, you should imagine how you want to depict the three categories on your website to appeal to customers and demonstrate what you offer which customers in which market.

DERIVATION (STEPS 1 TO 3)

CHANGED BENEFIT FEATURE	EFFECT ON OFFERING	CUSTOMER SEGMENT	MARKET	POTENTIAL	LEVEL OF LOSS (Risk)	PROBABILITY (Risk)

TARGET MARKETS

COURSE OF ACTION (STEPS 4 AND 5)

	REDUCE OFFERING	EXISTING OFFERING	MODIFIED OFFERING	NEW OFFERING	FUTURE OFFERING
MARKET REDUCTION	**1.** **Retreat:** Reduction of offerings and market presence	**2.** **Product-constant market consolidation:** Offer existing offerings in fewer markets			
EXISTING MARKETS	**3.** **Market-constant product consolidation:** Reduction of offering portfolio in existing markets	**4.** **Market penetration:** Gain additional market share with marketing activities	**5.** **Product modification:** An existing product is modified, the resulting value added induces the existing target group to make a repeat purchase	**6.** **Product development:** Developing a product further can induce established customers to make new purchases	**12.** **Offering identification:** Identification of future offerings for existing and familiar markets
FAMILIAR MARKETS		**7.** **Market expansion:** Existing products are sold to the familiar target group in new geographic markets	**8.** **Limited diversification:** Existing products are adapted to new geographic markets and modified for them	**9.1.** **Partial diversification I:** New products are developed for different requirements of new geographic markets	
NEW CUSTOMER SEGMENTS		**10.** **Market development:** Development of new, e.g., regional markets to increase revenue from existing products	**9.2.** **Partial diversification II:** Products are modified according to new requirements of new customer segments	**11.** **Diversification:** horizontal, vertical, lateral	Future offerings for future markets/target groups
FUTURE MARKETS/ CUSTOMER SEGMENTS		**13.** **Market identification:** Identification of future markets for existing and modified offerings		**14.** **Future diversification:** New future offerings for future markets/target groups	

NOTE

If one of your decisions falls on course of action number 12, 13 or 14, the "Experiment" process step might possibly help you process this potential "blue ocean". In that process step, you can follow the recommended tasks then return to this point in the workflow again.

CUSTOMER SEGMENTS

DECISIONS (STEP 6)

PRIORITIZATION (1–7)	COURSE OF ACTION	DO	EXAMINE	WATCH

OFFERINGS

FORMULATE YOUR PLAYING FIELD

OBJECTIVES & KEY RESULTS

DO WHAT REALLY COUNTS

"Dreams without goals are just dreams. And ultimately, they fuel disappointment. On the road you must apply discipline, but more importantly, consistency. Because without commitment you'll never start, but without consistency, you'll never finish."

Denzel Washington, US actor

What are the most important things that your organization must tackle to realize the target vision with "impact statement", "customer benefit & superior profits" and "playing field"?

In the final step of Strategy Workshop I, you have to define your strategic priorities. These are the critical factors that make the biggest difference to the success of your strategy. The longer the list of priorities, the slimmer the chance that you will even complete one of them.

SET THE RIGHT PRIORITIES

The objectives and key results will determine how you will mobilize the resources and skills available in your company to realize the target vision. As soon as the overarching objectives have been defined, they should be communicated throughout the organization. Essentially, this means breaking down the target vision onto the various levels, functions, and people within the organization. We go into this breakdown process in detail in the "Cascade" process step.

"Objectives & Key Results"

The greatest challenge for strategists lies in implementing and executing the strategy once it has been formulated. Let us turn our strategy power into implementation motion. To do this, we will use a tried and tested management method: "OKR = Objectives & Key Results" – combining objectives with key results, because "implementation is everything. (...) There are so many people working so hard and achieving so little," venture capitalist John Doerr (2018) states in his book, *Measure what matters*. Doerr got to know OKR as an employee at Intel and later introduced the OKR concept successfully as a venture capitalist at start-ups he supported, like Google. However, it is also suitable for large, complex organizations.

OKRS IN THE STRATEGY PROCESS

OKRs are a management instrument for objective-based steering of companies, teams, or individual people. The origins of OKRs can be found in Peter Drucker's famous "management by objectives" approach, which revolutionized corporate management in the 1950s but in its practical implementation also revealed weaknesses, for example, incentives to realize individual objectives to the detriment of overarching objectives. To eradicate these weaknesses, the co-founder and longstanding CEO of Intel, Andy Grove, refined the approach by introducing the key results. These are objectively measurable criteria (for example, revenue growth) which show the degree to which the objective has been achieved.

The magic of the OKRs emerges through consistency of application. There is a disciplined cycle with a meeting routine that has been adapted to the objective in question to examine and sustain ("tracking") progress.

Correct tracking is important to create transparency about who is pursuing which objectives, where each one stands and what all objectives together are paying into.

Knowing what your own contribution to achieving a shared, higher objective entails, on the one hand contributes to giving the executives or employees involved a sense of purpose. On the other hand, it is important for consistent pursuit of the objective. In reality this is more difficult than it sounds because ultimately it is about sticking to the guidelines and keeping track of their implementation.

In a strategy context, the OKRs that must be set should not be thought of in terms of the frequently prevailing quarterly logic. If you only have 3-month objectives embedded in the main strategy, it can subsequently be difficult because implementation also takes time. For that reason, an expanded temporal range for certain objectives definitely makes sense. Stretch goals can have a time frame of 2 to 3 years, while mid-term goals ("moals") are generally geared to one year. In a subsequent step, the stretch goals or moals can be translated into ambitious 3-month OKR sets to sort the measures you need to develop into the action areas. This enables you to use the OKRs to build a bridge from the target vision to the action areas where targeted measures can be planned with adequate deployment of resources.

The success of a strategy implementation process often depends on cascading the canon of objectives from corporate level down to the levels below, and particularly to the various business fields. Depending on the size and complexity of the enterprise this can be a very difficult undertaking that frequently can only be managed with software support nowadays. However, the OKRs will support the content management if they display the desired impact, the objectives being pursued and the planned measures with their time frames.

ADAPTABILITY WITH OKRS

Critics often find strategy processes lacking in room for agile and flexible action. Once a strategy is selected, it is not written in stone. This is where OKRs develop an important additional benefit. On the one hand, they create a commitment to action, but on the other hand they permit flexibility. This steering instrument opens up the opportunity to adapt certain elements of the strategy without having to change the entire strategy.

You should ask these questions at least once every quarter: How far along are we in achieving our objectives? Are the objectives we have set still the right ones, or do we need to adjust them? Consistent, institutionalized examination and adjustment of the OKRs using the meeting routines improve the implementation of the strategy. That is how you turn the power of your strategy into implementation motion.

OKRs also give space to all involved. In the target spaces, that were developed 60 percent top-down and 40 percent bottom-up and agreed jointly with the team and at individual level, you create a very binding, shared system. That is why it is important that this objective system is transparent to everyone. That means: They know their colleagues' objectives. They also pay into a shared team objective. If everyone only pursues individual objectives that are not connected to each other, it is questionable whether this is the right way and whether it can take the undertaking forward. The strength to implement the strategy successfully lies in your team. For example, you need resources from the IT team to move forward with the digitalization process. You can only do so much in your own department if the support from the IT team is not foreseen in the objective. Then problems arise in resource allocation. OKRs can also facilitate resource deployment because you do not get caught up in the minutia of the measures anymore, but instead you capture the value contribution of the individual measures and examine their purpose and contribution to the strategy.

SAMPLE SET

OBJECTIVE 1: Grow into the leading international provider of XYZ.

KEY RESULT 1: We will increase our revenue outside Germany by EUR 80 million.

KEY RESULT 2: We will gain 500 new B2B customers for our basic product.

KEY RESULT 3: Time from development investment to finished product reduced by 2 years on average.

OBJECTIVE 2: Accelerate our customers' sustainable transformation.

KEY RESULT 1: We will reduce the carbon footprint of our products by at least 10 percent.

KEY RESULT 2: 50 percent of our employees are trained in the new ESG taxonomy.

KEY RESULT 3: 40 percent reduction in the fuel consumption of our vehicle fleet.

OBJECTIVE 3: Create an amazing place to work.

KEY RESULT 1: Cut voluntary employee resignations to 3 percent.

KEY RESULT 2: Increase employee satisfaction to 50 eNPS.

KEY RESULT 3: Increase new applicant numbers to 200.

OBJECTIVES & KEY RESULTS

It is time to set your objectives to make your strategy measurable in its implementation and results. Don't shy away from it. Without this steering element in the target vision, everything else is building castles in the air.

KEY QUESTIONS:

1. Which objectives do we want to pursue in the strategy time frame?

2. What will make the biggest difference if we do it differently tomorrow?

3. What are our top priorities?

4. What is the lever of our success? And how is it measured?

INSTRUCTIONS

1. Every workshop participant writes down their personal top priorities individually on cards. Share the collected priorities in the group.
2. Cluster these and vote on which topics (maximum of 5!) you want to formulate objectives for.
3. Formulate three to five ambitious qualitative objectives with your team.
4. Formulate two to five measurable key results for each objective
   a. Participant number lower than 10: in the entire group
   b. Participant number from 10: in breakout groups
5. Transfer your final objectives and key results into the visible page in the StrategyFrame®.
6. Tracking, meeting routines and cycles for sustaining momentum will be defined at a later time as part of the entire strategy workflow.

CAUTION

- Do not confuse qualitative objectives with measurable key results!
- Set the bar high, higher, a little higher still! If you can achieve your objectives easily, you may miss the unique opportunity to really take your company to the next level.
- Do not confuse key results with specific implementation measures.
- Every key result must be measurable and trackable. If it is not measurable, it is not a key result!

COLLECT

CUSTOMER SEGMENT

OBJECTIVES

1.

2.

3.

4.

5.

KEY RESULTS

OBJECTIVES & KEY RESULTS

FORMULATE OBJECTIVES & KEY RESULTS

PLAN YOUR NEXT STEPS

"There is always a next game!"

Sepp Herberger, former iconic head coach of the German national soccer team (World Champion 1954)

After you have filled the first two pillars of the StrategyFrame® with your team, you will have almost reached the end of Strategy Workshop I. Maybe you are not yet 100 percent satisfied with each and every formulation. But at least the workshop should have inspired you and your team for the next steps. However, when you return to day-to-day company business, be prepared for questions or comments from your organization like: "So, what wonderful surprises have you decided this time then?" "Why weren't more people involved?" "When will we find out what was discussed?" "What will change for us?" "So, how was the mood?" "They were just off on a junket at the company's expense." Don't let yourself be provoked! Of course, you should have one or two responses to hand. How will you speak to your employees about the workshop? And what happens next? You should find concrete answers to these questions before the end of the workshop.

PUT IT IN A NUTSHELL

The first thing you should do is make the following clear to the workshop participants: What we wrote down together has to be digested now and can still change. Your strategy's new language will immediately create a new reality for everyone in your team. Or as Italian movie director and screenwriter Federico Fellini determined: *"A different language is a different vision of life."* But this language and the content that was developed are only known to a very small circle up to now. And that should stay like that for the moment.

Take the time to question, test and linguistically refine or maybe even semantically refine the formulations from the StrategyFrame®. Ask your central process manager to organize this revision process so that there is no rewriting of what was jointly agreed behind closed doors. Since there is probably no one in the strategy team with the professional skills of a creative copywriter or even of an author, it makes sense to call in someone with these qualities for support with the formulations and the linguistic fine-tuning. As soon as the reformulations have been agreed with the strategy sponsor, you should talk these changes through with the workshop team, comparing each version against the other. Although this procedure is intensive, you will discover that every word and every formulation can trigger emotions. You should therefore handle textual adjustments with circumspection. Take 2 to 4 hours' time for this final process.

CREATE A POSITIVE PERCEPTION

"Perception matters ..." and "information travels faster than light". Everyone in the organization will know first-hand or through the office grapevine: There was a workshop with the management team, and something will have been decided there. How your organization speaks about the strategy process is something you can influence. What is decisive is what those involved in the strategy process as well as the remainder of the organization perceive – and how they perceive it. Create a positive perception through open and honest communication. At this time, you only have to communicate transparently the things that are directly relevant to the respective level in the company. Talk about the workshop and its participants openly in meetings and maybe even in a media format like your internal social media channel using a striking and symbolically powerful photo of the workshop event and its participants. However, you should not make any reference to the content of the situation analysis or the target vision you developed. After all, your strategy is only two-thirds ready. Provide clarity and certainty by explaining the next process steps to all employees. What exactly are the next steps, who will be informed when about what, who will be involved when and how? That sounds banal, but if people know when they can expect what, and if there is fundamental trust in the reliability of your statements, then even those who tend to presume the worst will calm down.

Only communicate what is relevant

PRESENT PERSPECTIVES

Communicate to the members of the broader management team when they will learn about the content of Strategy Workshop I and how they will be involved. If you haven't done it yet, now at the latest time you should start planning Strategy Workshop II with a clear key question and sending out invitations: What exactly will we tackle? Of course, the fact that the next management levels will now be involved is also important information for all the other employees of your company. It sends a signal that you are proceeding methodically and proportionately. That generates trust. Ideally, you should also communicate a date for when you want to present the new strategy to the entire workforce and the format you want to use to do it with. If you want to get the organization on board, in our experience it is often enough just to state: "At the end of the month of ... we will present our new strategy to you and demonstrate how you can all contribute to its success." We recommend that you agree on the communication procedure during the workshop. Speak with one voice as a management team and send clear messages.

NEXT STEPS

At the end of Strategy Workshop I, you should answer the key questions about communication as well as about planning the process. That will give your top management team certainty for dealing with the topic in the workforce and clarity about the next steps.

KEY QUESTIONS:

ON COMMUNICATION:

1. When and how will you speak with your employees about the workshop?

2. Will there be official communication about the workshop in existing meeting formats and media channels?

3. What are the key messages?

ON THE ROADMAP:

1. When will you vote on the final content from Strategy Workshop I again together as a team?

2. When will Strategy Workshop II on the action areas take place? Who will attend this workshop?

3. When and how do you want to present the entire StrategyFrame® to your employees?

INSTRUCTIONS

1. Answer the key questions with the help of the template on the right.

2. Plan the next milestones and check these against your entire master plan from the "Plan" process step.

3. Transfer the milestones.

TIP

- Do not distribute the StrategyFrame® from Strategy Workshop I to the participants after the workshop.
- Do not spread the content to broader management teams or the workforce.
- Explain the future process procedure openly.
- Let emotionalizing photos from the workshop speak for themselves.

CORE MESSAGES

_____
_____
_____
_____
_____

PUBLICATION (internal)

MEDIUM/MEETING	TARGET GROUP	CONTENT (TEXT IMAGE)	DATE	COMMENT

STRATEGY WORKSHOP II (1.5 days)

**Which should be involved in the next step
(depending on management levels and the size of the company)?**

Management level: _____

Management level: _____

Management level: _____

Number of participants: _____

Venue: _____   Date: ___.___._____

CHECKLIST FOR FORMULATING THE KEY MESSAGES

☐ Only one language is used (no foreign terms or sentences).

☐ No catchphrases or internal jargon.

☐ Conventional spelling throughout.

☐ Sequence of core messages creates a consistent, logical and understandable story.

☐ The urgent need for change that follows on from the situation analysis and the challenges identified is also palpable emotionally.

☐ The target image has a radiating effect and is motivating.

"LIFE BELONGS TO THE LIVING, AND HE WHO LIVES MUST BE PREPARED FOR CHANGE."

Johann Wolfgang von Goethe, German poet

ADAPT

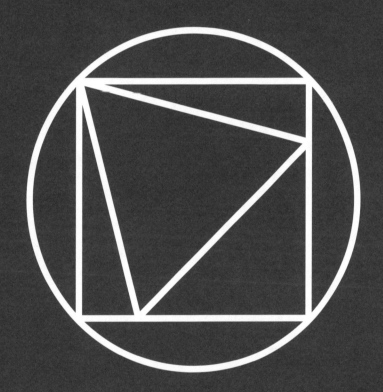

WHAT WE ARE TACKLING

"You must do the thing you think you cannot do."
Eleanor Roosevelt, former US human rights activist, diplomat, and First Lady

You and your management team now know where you stand and where you want to take your company. As the next step, you need to gear and adapt your organization to the company's strategic environment you have defined. Adaptation means "adjustment". We understand that to mean the various processes that have a combined effect of making your company form a responsive system for the external forces with which the desired target vision can be realized.

Adaptation implies:

> - questioning and adjusting the current "structures and processes",
> - checking if the right "people" with the right skills are on board or if human resources need to be relocated, augmented, or overhauled,
> - reviewing your company's "culture" critically because, as Peter Drucker stated trenchantly: "culture eats strategy for breakfast",
> - making your "data & IT" future-proof,
> - ensuring that "innovation" is not an unfamiliar concept and your organization does not suffer from "not invented here" syndrome but instead continuously confronts new developments and advances these itself, and, finally,
> - having the right "partners" at your side for key topics.

If you want to move your entire organization in the desired direction you have to tweak a lot of buttons simultaneously. You suspect or you know from experience: That is no easy task. Four points are crucial for the successful implementation of your plan:

Tweaks for adapting the organization

> 1. You adapt your entire corporate system. Irrespective of which initiatives, projects or measures you might start: They have to contribute to achieving the objectives you determined. Pursue these with tireless consistency and precisely regulated responsibilities.
> 2. You have a clear roadmap with the right dramaturgy to overcome resistance and accelerate change.
> 3. You generate a progressive perception of success for your plan with a concise and convincing "storyline" with which you, your fellow executives and selected multipliers communicate the overall strategy picture to the organization through an adequate communication infrastructure.

CLOSE GAPS

Operationalize your objectives and key results and fill them out with initiatives, projects, and measures. To do this, you need a translation into the language for going down the path that should lead you to the realization of your target vision. You should therefore transform your objectives with their key results into gap statements that describe the current and the desired future state of the organization for each objective. From these you can derive the obstacles that must be overcome to realize the desired future.

In this way, you will create an understanding for the reality of your shared strategy journey and enable progress to be measured, obstacles to be eliminated and successes to be celebrated. You will put the strategic agenda into the spotlight with specified initiatives, projects, and measures as well as defined time frames. Hand over responsibility to your management team for closing the gaps across all the objectives. This will also prevent a potential silo mentality which will emerge at the latest when you are "cascading" the strategy into the individual business areas, departments, and teams. Install one main manager per objective from your management team. This will make progress measurable. You will not get lost in the minutiae of endless reporting meetings, Excel sheets or complicated program management landscapes.

Prevent silos

GEAR YOUR BUSINESS SYSTEM TO THE STRATEGY

Although closing the gaps is of decisive importance, it is not enough. For your strategy to lead to success, all the elements of your organization's action system must be effectively geared to this strategy. The existing organization embodies the action system for yesterday's strategy. Now the system has to be aligned with the strategy for tomorrow.

An organization's action system must function holistically, like an ecosystem where each part supports the other parts. Strategy needs consistency – the elements must fit together like the pieces of a jigsaw – and coherence – all activities must dovetail into one another like the cogs in a clock movement. If one single element does not play its supporting role or if the elements work against each other, your strategy will get bogged down. To ensure this does not happen, you must process the six elements of your action system as action areas:

1. STRUCTURES & PROCESSES

What do you have to adapt structurally and process-wise? This is not just about structures and processes as a whole and overall, but also in the individual units (like departments). For example, a new sales approach can make it necessary to change from the classic sales model to an e-commerce model which requires new structures and processes.

What does your process landscape look like? Are your current processes documented comprehensibly? What do the processes that are ideal for tomorrow look like? How can you design these "end to end", automate them if necessary, and implement them?

2. PEOPLE

Do you have the right team with the right competencies on board? Are your management levels filled with the right people? Do you have clearly defined roles, responsibilities, and hierarchies? Where do you have to expand, reduce, or relocate resources? Are new competencies needed? What training course or coaching do your employees need to get to the level that is relevant for your strategy?

Nothing works without the human resource. In an aging and shrinking society, this resource is becoming increasingly scarce and the market therefore increasingly competitive. It stopped being just a "war for talent", a battle for new recruits, a long time ago. Increasingly frequently and in future probably to an even greater extent, employees must take on changing tasks and roles. Finding capable and motivated employees, and especially keeping them, is a challenge. How are you facing this challenge? Is your company attractive enough as an employer, or does it need new incentives? Have you institutionalized employee development? Is there a talent pool? How do you foster this? Is there a succession management program?

3. CULTURE

Are your corporate, management and work cultures suitable for realizing your strategic target vision? What values are your actions based on? How much "boss and subordinates" thinking is in your management culture? Do you have an error culture? Can a "cooperative management system" make it easier to achieve your objectives? Do you need stronger self-management or decentralization? What role do "New Work elements" play?

You should ask yourself these questions – and probably a few more as well – because the action area is very diverse. As diverse as your company. Sit down with your team and think about what sort of management is necessary for tomorrow and how the cooperative process should be designed.

4. DATA & IT

Nothing works without a digital backbone anymore. Is your IT infrastructure future-proof? Have you set up your system landscape for the future? Do you need to harmonize your system and application landscape so that you can manage the various parts of the company better? Do you need specific digital solutions to achieve the objectives you have set?

But it does not stop at software and hardware systems. What do you actually do with your data? Nothing, a bit, or have you already been gripped by collecting mania? What about your data structure? Are screws given a different inventory number per business unit in every ERP system? Have you established a master data management system?

5. INNOVATION

Is innovation hardwired into your organization's DNA, or is it a foreign concept? How do you deal with trends? Do you manage them actively, or does only your research and development department handle them? How do you identify new trends, and how are these incorporated into new product development? Is there a systematic process for this? How do you measure your innovation capacity? How much money do you invest in the future survival of your company?

6. PARTNERS

Companies are now foregoing cooperation with other companies to protect assumed competitive advantages. In this case, because of secretiveness and fearing a loss of control, companies prefer to do everything themselves although they would have been able to take advantage of cost-cutting or value-enhancing complementarities in a cooperative arrangement. Without openness to cooperation, the complexity of today's world cannot be overcome anymore.

Do you cooperate with other companies across your value chain? Do you have the right partners? What will you still do yourself in the future, and what will you buy in from other companies or service providers? Who do you want to cooperate with?

ACCELERATE CHANGE AND CREATE A PERCEPTION OF SUCCESS

After the action areas have been filled, you now have to draw up a roadmap. Kotter's (2014) approach with its eight accelerators of change has proved to be practicable. Your task is not to draw up a detailed plan of your "transformation", but to set a general course and also determine the right dramaturgy to eliminate resistance and build a network of supporters strategically. You will not develop a comprehensive and in-depth implementation concept until you reach the "Transformation" process step.

As soon as you have completed this process step with your team, you face the task of meeting your stakeholders (shareholders, investors, all management executives, and of course all employees) where they are at, convincing them of your plan and getting them on board for the strategy journey. Because of this, planning your communication takes on a key role.

With the StrategyFrame® you have already laid the foundation for the content of a storyline that will make the connections transparent and provide clarity on the "why". But it is not enough to simply distribute the StrategyFrame®. An entire potpourri of communication measures is required to gather your team behind the new strategy.

"ORGANIZATIONS ARE COMMUNITIES OF HUMAN BEINGS, NOT COLLECTIONS OF HUMAN RESOURCES."

Henry Mintzberg, management theorist and strategy pioneer

STRATEGYFRAME®

SITUATION ANALYSIS

CUSTOMERS

MARKET

COMPETITION

TRENDS

BROADER ENVIRONMENT

OWN REALITIES

CHALLENGE

TARGET VISION

IMPACT STATEMENT

CUSTOMER BENEFIT

TARGET MARKETS

CUSTOMER SEGMENT

OBJECTIVES

ACTION AREAS

STRUCTURES & PROCESSES

PEOPLE

SUPERIOR PROFITS

CULTURE

DATA & IT

OFFERINGS

INNOVATION

PARTNERS

OBJECTIVE 1

OBJECTIVE 2

OBJECTIVE 3

OBJECTIVE 4

OBJECTIVE 5

KEY RESULTS

ROADMAP

STRATEGY WORKSHOP II

The second strategy workshop should take place about 4 to 6 weeks after the first workshop and after the final linguistic reformulation of the insights. This will enable you to keep the momentum going and close the gaps to the action areas.

KEY QUESTIONS & TIPS:

1. When and where will the strategy workshop be held?

In our experience, a time lag of 4 to 6 weeks after Workshop I is ideal. Remember to send out an invitation in good time to the broader management team. We recommend that you go "offsite" for this workshop as well and therefore leave your familiar habitat to create mental space to think and act.

2. How long should the strategy workshop take?

You should plan for 1.5 days to have enough time to get the new participants on board, identify gaps and develop suitable measures. As for Strategy Workshop I, we recommend starting the evening beforehand, eating dinner together and then hitting the ground running the next day.

3. Who should participate in the strategy workshop?

To make sure you don't just stew in your own juice, we recommend expanding the circle of participants deliberately to 20 to 30 people. Then you can work in five breakout groups across the five objectives with four to six participants per group. When you are expanding the circle, avoid getting too many worrywarts around the table. Instead, concentrate on initiators who will subsequently be able to act in a kind of strategic network and lend additional acceleration to the strategy process.

4. Who will be moderating the strategy workshop?

The task of the five objective teams is to develop targeted measures. You can pass over team responsibility to the experienced colleagues from your management team or from Workshop I. Then the strategy sponsor in tandem with the strategy process manager can take over moderation and coordination. Experience in working with this size of group is a clear advantage here. Of course, you can also call in an external moderator, especially if you would like to contribute yourself to developing the content in one of the objective teams.

DAY 1 ___.___._____ Duration about 3.5 hours + Evening meal

TIME	MODULE	FORMAT	EQUIPMENT	WHO	WHERE	RECOMMENDATION
___:___	Arrival and check-in					
___:___	Welcome address			Strategy sponsor	Conference room	15 mins.
___:___	**Check-in:** Participants from Workshop I: What inspired you in Workshop I?	Collect comments in a huddle	Metaplan board		Conference room	1 min. each (max. 15 mins.)
___:___	**Check-in:** New participants: What are your expectations for the workshop?	Collect comments in a huddle	Metaplan board		Conference room	1 min. each (max. 15 mins.)
___:___	**Presentation of StrategyFrame® I:** Situation analysis	Presentation	Projector or screen	Six participants from Workshop I	Conference room	10 mins per module (60 mins. in total)
___:___	Coffee break					15 mins.
___:___	**Presentation of StrategyFrame® II:** : Target vision	Presentation	Projector or screen	Strategy sponsor	Conference room	30 mins.
___:___	**Q&A session**	Collect questions in analog or digital format	Metaplan board	Participants from Workshop I answer questions	Conference room	30 mins.
___:___	**Outlook Day II:**	Presentation of Day II agenda	Projector or screen	Moderator	Conference room	15 mins.
___:___	**Check-out:** What surprised you today?			All participants	Conference room	15 mins.
___:___	Team dinner			All participants		

DAY 2 ___.___.___ all day

TIME	MODULE	FORMAT	EQUIPMENT	WHO	WHERE	RECOMMENDATION
___:___	Welcome address			Moderator	Conference room	5 mins.
___:___	**Check-in:** What is your plan for today?			All participants	Conference room	20 to 30 mins.
___:___	**Presentation of procedure**	Presentation	Projector or screen	Moderator	Conference room	15 mins.
___:___	**Assignment of participants to five breakout groups**		Projector or screen	Four to six people per group + objective leader	Conference room	5 mins.
___:___	Coffee break					15 mins.
___:___	**Identify gaps**	Work session	1 projector or screen per room + flipchart + 2 Metaplan boards	Assigned groups	Group rooms	45 mins.
___:___	**Present gaps**	Presentation		Objective leaders	Conference room	10 mins. per group
___:___	Lunch break					60 mins.
___:___	**Close gaps**	Work session	Action area maps	Assigned groups	Group rooms	45 mins.
___:___	**Gear organization to objective**	Work session	Action area maps	Assigned groups	Group rooms	45 mins.
___:___	Coffee break					15 mins.
___:___	**Present initiatives, projects and measures**	Presentation	Action area maps	Objective leaders	Conference room	10 mins. presentation and 5 mins. questions per group
___:___	**Prioritize measures**	Digital or analog vote	Five ratings points per participant	All participants	Conference room	5 mins.
___:___	**Transfer into action areas of StrategyFrame®**			Moderator	Conference room	5 mins.

TIME	MODULE	FORMAT	EQUIPMENT	WHO	WHERE	RECOMMENDATION
___:___	**Outlook for next process steps**	Present communication to all employees and cascade		Moderator	Conference room	10 mins.
___:___	**Feedback and check-out**	Collect in digital and analogformat	Metaplan board	All participants	Conference room	30 mins.
___:___	**Thank-you and farewell speech**			Strategy sponsor	Conference room	15 mins.

SET-UP IN THE GROUP ROOM

METAPLAN BOARD I

"Current state"

FLIPCHART

"Objective
1 to 5"
"Obstacles"

METAPLAN BOARD II

"Target state"

OBJECTIVE LEADER

PARTICIPANTS

TACKLE ACTION AREAS

What do you want to address specifically? How will you gear your entire organization to the new strategy? How can potential obstacles be overcome?

KEY QUESTIONS:

1. To what extent is the "current state" of our organization suitable for achieving the "objective"?

2. What will the "target state" of our organization look like when we have achieved the "objective"?

3. Which "obstacles" do we have to remove to reach the "target state"?

4. Which initiatives, projects and measures do we have to launch with which deadline to close the gap?

5. Looking at our organization's six action areas, what do we have to change with specific initiatives, projects, and measures to gear the organization to the objective?

INSTRUCTIONS

1. Please make as many copies of the action area map with the front and back pages as you have objectives or use the download function to work digitally.

2. Write your objective into the work page of the action area map or transfer it to a flipchart. Explain or add to the key results for the objective.

3. As a team, describe the "current state" of the organization. Write down the individual descriptions and attributes on the map or the Metaplan board.

4. As a team, describe the "target state": how the organization will look when the objective is achieved. Write down the individual descriptions and attributes on the map or the Metaplan board.

5. Derive the gaps between the "current state" and the "target state" by getting every participant to write down potential obstacles for achieving the objective on a card and pinning it up.

6. Develop creative solutions for how you want to overcome these obstacles with initiatives, projects, and measures. Classify these into the six action areas of your business system.

7. In the last step of your group work, add to the action areas the initiatives, projects, and measures that you have to change on the individual parameters to gear your business system to the strategy completely. You can also put existing measures into these categories if they already pay into the new strategy.

8. The entire group now votes on the most important measures for each objective and action area. Every participant gets five votes.

9. Now please transfer the selected initiatives, projects, and measures into the appropriate action areas in the frame.

TIP

When you are working in small groups, you should use the action area map or set up two Metaplan boards for the group work, one for the "current state" and one for the "target state" of your organization. Between them you can set up a flipchart on which you write the objective you worked on and list underneath it the obstacles you identified in the work session.

If an "objective" is too abstract for processing in the group, you should use the "key results" you have defined.

You can use the action area map for listing the initiatives, projects, and measures across the six action areas of the organization (digital or analog). Alternatively, you could use more sides of a Metaplan board.

ACTION AREAS

Objective: _____

Leader: _____

STRUCTURES & PROCESSES

PEOPLE

CULTURE

DATA & IT

INNOVATION

PARTNERS

NOTES

ROADMAP II FOR COMMUNICATION

GENERATE MOMENTUM FOR THE NEW DEPARTURE

"The single biggest problem with communication is the illusion that it has taken place."
George Bernard Shaw, Irish playwright and politician

The action areas have been filled in. You have released the subservient strategy genie from their bottle, but that does not mean that it has been accepted within the organization. Now the magic word is strategy communication. You have to spread the "good news": We have a new plan. You will tell your shareholders, employees, and other interest groups (investors, analysts, banks, …) where you are headed. That initially sounds like a one-way street, like "top-down" and, "We're talking, you'll listen and implement". But it's not that easy. Not everyone will instantly get all fired up about what you have developed with your management team and internal multipliers, because a new strategy means change. And the prospect of change stokes fears, particularly among employees, of being put on the "reject" pile and left behind. You therefore have to do a lot of convincing and win over the stakeholders to your plan. It should not come as a surprise to anyone nowadays that communication is the key to successful mediation and implementation. Unfortunately, the reality often looks different. A dialog idealistically envisaged to involve all participants quickly turns into a monologue that trails off at the second management level and never reaches the lower echelons of corporate headquarters. That is why you need a plan here, too, for how you want to get the "storyline" of the new strategy across to the entire workforce.

STORIES FROM THE FIELD

One of the authors of this book was invited some time ago to attend a strategy meeting with the CEO of a large company. The top manager talked enthusiastically about the new strategy that had evolved in collaboration with external consultants and was currently being implemented. It all sounded well thought-out, plausible given the company's situation at the time, and intrinsically coherent. As luck would have it, the co-author encountered a senior manager from the company's strategy department in the lobby after the meeting. They knew each other from before. The co-author said the CEO had just given him a presentation about the new corporate strategy. He got a surprising response: "A new strategy? That's the first time I have heard of it…" A few weeks later, two middle managers from the same company were attending a training event run by the co-author. Naturally, the co-author asked: "So, how is the new strategy working out?" Answer: "What new strategy?" Ponderous silence. "Do you mean our new TV commercials, maybe?"

FROM DEVELOPMENT TO IMPLEMENTATION

You are currently in a transition phase from strategy development to implementation. This is a sore point in the strategy process because this is where the dynamics of the process change fundamentally. While you were always on top of the situation in the strategy development phase and could dictate the dramaturgy clearly for a manageable scope of people, the rules of the game are changing now. You should now have a clear idea about who you want to put into the picture, and how and when. But we have three pieces of good news before you start: Firstly, you already have familiarized politically important people with the process through elements like the qualitative interviews. Secondly, you have been continually updating your workforce in your communication on the first process steps about the progress of the process and sensitized them to the necessity of a new strategy and the change it entails. And thirdly, the StrategyFrame® provides you with a basis for your strategy narrative and an instrument for subsequent communication and persuasion.

COMMUNICATE THE OVERALL PICTURE

StrategyFrame® = storyline

It is important that you communicate the overall picture. Instead of countless tedious PowerPoint slides, the StrategyFrame® presents your analysis results as well as the shared interpretations and decisions of the strategy team on the three pillars: "Where do we stand?", "Where do we want to go?" and "What do we have to tackle?" in a structured, clear, and contextualized format. This gives you the structure for the story you want to tell, the content for this story and the screenplay of how you want to tell your story. To borrow a movie phrase: The storyline is done. Now you have to answer the following questions: Who do you want to make enthusiastic about your strategy, and when, in what format, and with which core messages?

1. ADAPT CONTENT & VISUALS

Examine the content of the StrategyFrame® from this point of view: Is the strategy portrayed in a clear and comprehensible way to all involved or all affected? Are the selected formulations succinct?

Will you thin out content some more to make the core of the strategy easier and better to grasp? For this, it can be helpful to visually adapt the StrategyFrame® to your corporate design, your corporate colors and your logo, or even to a strong motif for the background. However, you should keep the basic structure because this helps you make a compelling line of argument.

2. SELECT THE TARGET GROUPS AND TIMING

Decide who in your organization and in your environment must be informed when, how and about what. You must involve stakeholder groups, committees, and individuals with a strong interest in and influence on your undertaking at an early stage and constantly bring them up to date. You should keep stakeholders who either have a strong interest but little influence or a strong influence but little interest informed about your progress.

3. DEFINE THE CORE MESSAGES

Determine which core messages in the strategy are important to which target group. This will enable you to tailor the focus of your communication to each target group and the selected format.

4. DECIDE THE EVENT FORMATS

Which formats do you want to use to bring each of the target groups up to speed: Supervisory or advisory board meeting, capital markets day, investor briefing, bank meeting, executive meeting (if you have not yet involved all management levels in the process), works council or staff meeting, or digital strategy summit on the web? Select the formats that suit your company and are sure to get the appropriate attention.

If the selected media and event formats are to function, you will need a well-crafted dramaturgy. Ensure that information, dialog, and emotion are balanced. After all, you want to win over people to your plan. Information and explanation are indispensable if people are to understand your strategy. Dialog provides the opportunity to question and clarify what has been communicated. Set an emotional anchor that will convey the significance of the plan to the recipients of your strategy message through more than just "blood, sweat and tears" or a rationally driven line of argument. A very proficient guest speaker can work wonders here. If you think this type of support would make sense, make sure that this speaker establishes a link to your company's situation and to your strategy and does not merely reel off generalized motivational stories.

5. USE THE MEDIA

If you want to make your strategy known within your company and – if you wish – beyond it too, you should use what you have. And if you do not have much, this is the right time to build a clean media architecture within your company: intranet, employee newspaper, newsletters, videos. To help you make progress faster or as a complementary measure, you can of course avail of external communication in classic and social media as well.

6. DISTRIBUTE THE STRATEGYFRAME®

Use the StrategyFrame® in all formats as your visual anchor to prevent your audience from losing the thread. Visualize the connection for your employees between today – meaning your daily work routines – and the future expressed in the target vision. Distribute the StrategyFrame® to all employees and present it additionally at central locations in your company. Anything that is omnipresent will not disappear so lightly into a drawer.

7. SET UP A CENTRAL PLATFORM

Set up a central digital platform internally that displays the strategy content, process steps as well as the target and current states. This is for controlling the perception of success and particularly for creating transparency in project task completion and progress checks. To do this, you also have to cascade objectives, key results, and measures.

8. BE VISIBLE

Presenting a corporate strategy is the boss's job because there can be no strategy without leadership and no leadership without strategy. If you are not operating as a "lone wolf", then be sure to shine the stage lights on the other people involved in the strategy process as well. This will send a strong message that the entire management team supports the strategy.

9. ANNOUNCE MILESTONES AND LIGHTHOUSE MEASURES

It is not enough to have a broadly-based but one-off communication drive. It is time for the next two process steps. You should set clear starting and finishing dates for "cascading" the objectives and key results in your corporate functions and business areas or regions. You should also communicate the starting date for the "Transformation" now already.

COMMUNICATION PLANNING

DATE	TARGET GROUP	CORE MESSAGES	EVENT	MEDIA	PAYS INTO: 1. Information 2. Dialog 3. Emotion

MILESTONE PLANNING

Start of cascading process ___.___._____   End of cascading process ___.___._____

Start of transformation ___.___._____

with the following lighthouse measures: _____

_____

_____

_____

_____

_____

_____

ROADMAP II

"EXECUTION IS EVERYTHING."

John Doerr, OKR evangelist, investor and venture capitalist

CASCADE

ACHIEVE MORE TOGETHER

"What one cannot do alone, many can do together."
Friedrich Wilhelm Raiffeisen, German social reformer and municipal official

All key stakeholders are now in the picture about the new direction for your company. But you are not even halfway there when it comes to bringing your strategy to life. You will now start the strategy implementation process with the "Cascade" process step. After the Big Bang announcement "We're realigning our company!", a communication vacuum often develops if it is not immediately clear what that means and what the next steps will look like. You and your management team must now breathe life into your strategy tiger to ensure that it does not degenerate into a paper tiger in your day-to-day routines.

STUMBLING BLOCK NUMBER 1: IMPLEMENTATION!

According to Sull et al. (2019), 67 percent of all corporate strategies fail because of a lack of competence in implementation. Momentive (2022) surveyed 1,750 decision-makers in companies with more than 1,000 employees in the USA, the UK and Australia about dealing with and experience of strategy. The findings are catastrophic: "A sobering 9 out of 10 organizations fail to execute their strategy."

The reasons are manifold. However, the core of the problem is the difference in focus between the management level and the employees. Objectives are unclear, employees are frequently excluded from tracking the achievement of objectives (47 percent of all respondents). The frequency with which employees look at strategy varies from once a month (32 percent) to twice a year (30 percent), whereas 63 percent of top management executives look at strategy on a weekly basis. These are appalling figures if we think about the time and effort that was put into strategy development. But that is no reason to throw in your strategy towel.

GETTING YOUR POWER INTO IMPLEMENTATION MOTION

The most important thing you can do for your strategy – and the success of your company – and also the most difficult, is to put your plan into the hands of your management executives and employees. Many questions pop up around this, even after the best communication of the strategy using the StrategyFrame®: What does the strategy mean specifically to me? To my team? To my business area? How can we contribute to fulfilling the objectives? And what is my personal contribution?

The "cascading" will provide the answers. The term, which is used in different spheres like IT, electricity generation, or management, means achieving a greater effect with modules arranged in a succession of stages than with only one individual module or with modules that are operating totally detached from each other. While the connection between the individual modules is unidirectional, you can still trace back the connection to the start of the chain.

But how do we set in motion this chain reaction that will ignite your strategy and carry it throughout your company like the Olympic torch? You have to break down the big picture in a way that makes it meaningful and understandable for employees' day-to-day work. The bigger and more complex your company is, the greater the time and human resources effort required to cascade your objectives and key results. Matrix organizations pose an even greater challenge still, as the following example from the corporate playing field shows.

STORIES FROM THE FIELD

It shows in practice: Few people have a real overview of what is going on in a company. We are not painting a black picture here; this is bitter company reality. An international customer from the mobility sector was working with us on honing their group strategy, including the definition of the most value-adding activities across all divisions, regions, and countries. The management board, all division and function heads as well as the regional P&L controllers were involved. After weeks of grappling with the right objectives, figures, and formulations, they proudly presented the adapted track out of the strategy crisis to the internal workforce as well as the external investor audience. Everyone was excited and swore to uphold the agreed objectives, including the abandonment of a historically important but no longer profitable product segment.

But what then showed up month after month in the company's financial figures, particularly in one key market, was unfortunately a far cry from the expectations that had been formulated. After the region heads had wrestled with the country management and opened an investigation, they noticed that a completely new product line had been constructed for precisely this unprofitable product segment. The project had swallowed up enormous financial resources for investments and still continued to operate consistently in the red. But it was precisely this product segment that had been discontinued, dismantled, or disposed of in all other countries based on the agreed new strategy.

This example shows how important it is to cascade the strategy and the defined objectives correctly and to conduct progress checks for each objective. That is why you must lay the foundations you need for successful implementation. Do not let yourself be discouraged by complexity and effort to derive the objectives and key results from the StrategyFrame® through your entire company, fill them with specific leaders, measures, budgets and timelines, and make their implementation constantly measurable. This step is extremely important to your success.

1. DEFINE YOUR CASCADE

You will now say that it is patently obvious how the cascade is supposed to go – it will simply follow our existing hierarchy, our org chart – from top to bottom. But if you look closely, that is not so trivial at all.

Who will lead which cascade meeting with which hierarchy level and which number of participants? What is the time frame for when we should have penetrated into the farthest reaches of our company? How will we coordinate the objectives, key results and measures we have developed with the other teams on the horizontal level? Because in this phase it is not just about supporting the vertical team coordination on objectives and key results but also ensuring the horizontal coordination. Everyone will attempt to make their contribution, but maybe they won't be able to do it because they lack the support of another team. That promotes counterproductive silo mentalities. A good example of this would be support from the IT team for the digitalization of business areas or business units. You can have the most wonderful objectives that pay into the strategy, but if you do not synchronize them with the IT team, you will be waiting a long time for the implementation of your ambitious digital project. If objectives are not synchronized, there is a lack of resources and commitment. Frustration is high and the old familiar "blame game" begins.

For this reason, good, centralized planning and management of the strategy cascade rollout by the strategy process manager is a key success factor. Start the cascade for the overall undertaking with the two highest management levels 0 to 1. In smaller companies, management and team leaders are sufficient if you have no further management levels. Start deriving the objectives and key results from the StrategyFrame® for one year and then for one quarter. Subsequently you should plan your management level 1 or your team leaders from the SME example with their "direct reports" (management level 2 or employees in the SME example). Ideally, you should continue to build the cascade further downward until you have reached every employee in your organization.

However, it is not always advisable to go down to the last operational level. In no way does that mean that these people do not deserve to be involved in the process. However, it is not necessary for the colleagues in the mail room or at reception, for example, to have this type of target system on their plates. You should also make sure that the individual groups in the cascade do not encompass more than 15 people because otherwise you cannot ensure active participation from all members, and some will adopt a consumption mindset. In this case, you should preferably divide up the group and conduct the group meeting twice. You should also check that no staff position holders or special functions fall through the grid and are therefore not taken into account.

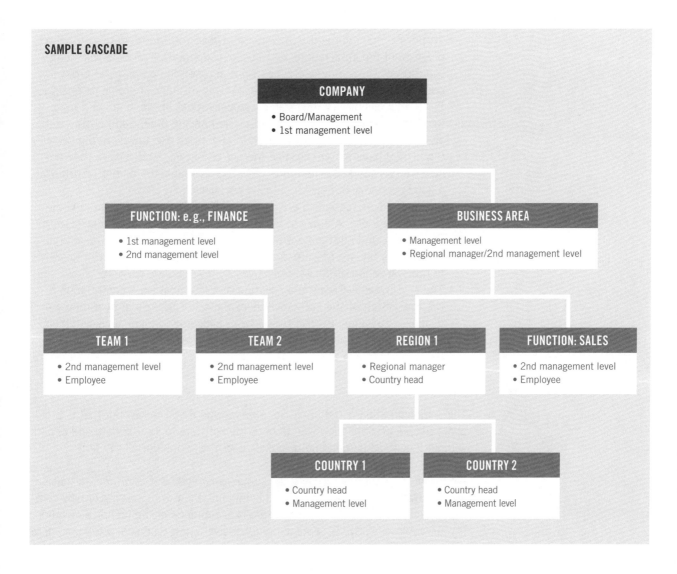

SAMPLE CASCADE

COMPANY
- Board/Management
- 1st management level

FUNCTION: e.g., FINANCE
- 1st management level
- 2nd management level

BUSINESS AREA
- Management level
- Regional manager/2nd management level

TEAM 1
- 2nd management level
- Employee

TEAM 2
- 2nd management level
- Employee

REGION 1
- Regional manager
- Country head

FUNCTION: SALES
- 2nd management level
- Employee

COUNTRY 1
- Country head
- Management level

COUNTRY 2
- Country head
- Management level

2. CREATE A CENTRAL PLATFORM

There is no doubt that, when it comes to breaking down objectives and regularly checking progress, there is no dearth of clever recommendations from the OKR method world and numerous tracking software solutions. There is something to suit everyone's taste: from intelligent PowerPoint to programmed Excel tables and beyond. Here, too, the trick is not to overdo it with the reporting, tracking, and controlling and nevertheless being able to observe the progress of the implementation on a central basis that is transparent to everyone. To do this, you have to consider various needs and wants:

- Corporate management will want to always retain an overview of the progress of the implementation, resource expenditure and the value contribution of the various activities right across the company, in order to be able to intervene if necessary, especially if financial problems arise.
- Those responsible for the strategy process must on the one hand maintain the "dashboard" for the overview and on the other hand ensure the activation of the employees involved through their executives. At the same time, they have to synchronize the set objectives and ensure they are consistently tracked. Therefore, the process managers do not just need a good overview, but also a detailed perspective.
- The executives responsible for the implementation must communicate the message of the new strategy consistently, derive the objectives for their teams and fill them out with feasible measures. From this point on, they will be under pressure and will have to show their hand with regard to the realization of the set objectives.
- The employees will want to know first and foremost what contribution to the realization of the objectives is expected of them and how they are supposed to handle the topics and tasks allocated to them alongside their daily business under the pressure of regular reporting and full transparency of individual performance.

This initial situation is definitely not an easy one if you remember that it is still about people who are supposed to populate software tools with data and results without feeling as if someone is looking over their shoulder all the time.

We therefore recommend using the project management instruments that are already available in the company and combining them with existing or new communication systems. The key word here is acceptance of the technical solution. If your employees have acceptance problems with new technical solutions, there is a danger that they will transfer this problem orientation onto their attitude to the new strategy and the entire process. Put the onus on your management team to explain the purpose of new tools to their own employees and to ask them individually about the implementation progress. It pays to take the time to do this. What is important is that you have the right direction and sentiment for your project.

3. CONDUCT STRATEGIC DIALOGS

Hone an understanding for how the strategy hangs together in dialogs with the different teams. Write down where the company stands today. Derive ambitious objectives and key results from the next target level up in each case. Synchronize these with the teams from which you need support to achieve the set objectives. Define specific measures with responsibilities and deadlines for the next quarter.

If possible, use existing and therefore familiar meeting formats for the entire cascade. Extend these timewise if necessary. Communicate the dates and content in good time. Strategy has to penetrate into employees' daily routines and become embedded in their thoughts and actions. That is the most important task for you and your management team. It cannot be delegated down. Now your leadership qualities are called for. Be visible, and always be open to your employees' reservations and problems. They will initially be preoccupied with themselves and wondering what the strategy means for them personally. Allay their psychological insecurity. Communicate the strategy content with clarity and conviction and with direct relevance for the dialog group in question. Specify how and by when you will collect employee feedback and make it transparent.

To achieve comprehensive implementation in a reasonable time frame, ensure your executives are "on track", will not delay the dialog dates in the prescribed time frame or not report feedback or results on time out of self-interest.

The suggested objectives developed in the strategic dialog will then be entered into an analog or digital document and made available to everyone. If one team's suggestions depend on the resources of other teams, they must be aligned with each other to ensure horizontal integration. The key results per level need not be perfectly quantified or qualified. However, the better they are aligned with each other, the better you can ensure that your company can achieve its set objectives. Those responsible for the strategy process will provide consistency and synchronization across all levels in a final vertical alignment process. The result will be a consistent package of objectives and key results for the next quarter. It will dictate the direction for everyone and thus form the core of the entire process. The package will be rounded off with the measures and responsibilities that have been defined.

MEASURING PROGRESS AND ESTABLISHING A ROUTINE

Transparency across all levels and between all teams is an essential key to success. Discipline and consistency in day-to-day work poses a major challenge. Since the process is modelled on an OKR system, there is a risk of degenerating into a real tracking and meeting frenzy. However, all the companies we observed in OKR processes demonstrated one thing: An excessively rigid approach does not fire enthusiasm, but instead generates a feeling of bureaucracy. Additionally, many employees find it difficult to associate their day-to-day tasks with the objectives. Because the question is legitimate: If I do something, isn't it supposed to pay into the strategy – but what has my answering administrative emails got to do with it? A lot! If you are unable to carry out important measures effectively because of poor workplace organization, this impacts on the achievability of your objectives and key results.

What frequency should you use for measuring progress? OKR rules talk about "weekly" and dealing with them in various meeting formats. However, we would tend to advise you to adopt a monthly rhythm to give your teams sufficient time to act. Then the fine-tuning should follow once every quarter and we will delve into this more specifically in the "Adjust" process step.

"IDEAS DON'T MAKE YOU RICH. THE CORRECT EXECUTION OF IDEAS DOES."

Felix Dennis, British writer and publisher

CASCADE

This section contains instructions and tips for conducting the entire cascading process in your role of strategy process manager as well as a fillable template for the individual strategic team dialog.

KEY QUESTIONS FOR THE STRATEGIC DIALOG:

1. Where do we want to be with our company in 20XX? What have we already achieved, and what still needs to be done?
2. What do our customers and colleagues expect from us?
3. What specific challenges is our team facing?
4. What contribution can we make as a team?
5. What do we have to do better or differently? What exactly do we plan to do?

INSTRUCTIONS

Strategy process manager

1. **Define the cascade:** Detail the cascade through your company in an Excel table with responsibilities, participants per deadline and execution date.
2. **Select a central platform:** Set up a central platform for communication and for collecting the objectives and key results, potential key measures as well as the subsequent progress tracking. Establish these before you begin implementation.
3. **Initiate the strategy cascade:** Kick off with team dialog at the top corporate level
   3.1. Derive the strategic objectives and key results for the current year.
   3.2. Derive the quarterly objectives and key results.
   3.3. Start the cascade by assigning management level 1.

Moderation executive

4. **Prepare team dialog:** Get ready for the team dialog.
5. **Conduct team dialog:** Carry out the team dialog.
6. **Follow-up team dialog:** Report the results for the next quarter through the agreed channel or on the specified platform.
7. **Synchronize results:** Ensure a horizontal and vertical alignment.
8. **Set a routine:** Agree on the monthly reporting routine and set the dates for all the quarterly meetings in the calendar.

Strategy process manager

9. **Manage the cascade implementation:** Maintain the overview of the entire process and solve problems and delays.

MATERIALS FOR THE TEAM DIALOG:

- StrategyFrame® as a printout or digital
- Flipchart
- Metaplan board
- Objectives and key results of the higher-level team in the cascade for the next quarter
- Team dialog objectives & action area map (see next page – please copy or print for 3 to 5 objectives)

KEY DATA STRATEGIC TEAM DIALOG

Team _____

Moderator _____

Participants _____

_____

_____

_____

_____

_____

ROUTINE

Monthly on: ___.___._____

Quaterly on: ___.___._____

AGENDA

TIME	MODULE	FORMAT	EQUIPMENT	RECOMMENDATION
___:___	Welcome and check-in			About 10 mins.
___:___	Where do we want to get to by 20XX?	Collect the statements from the team members	• Flipchart • StrategyFrame®	About 20 mins.
___:___	What do our customers and colleagues expect from us?	Present the target vision from the StrategyFrame® again	• StrategyFrame® • Metaplan board	About 20 mins.
___:___	What contribution will we make to the strategy in the next quarter? (1/2)	Collect specific challenges across the 6 fields in the situation analysis with team relevance	• Objectives and key results upper level	About 40 mins.
___:___	Coffee break			About 15 mins.
___:___	What contribution will we make to the strategy in the next quarter? (2/2)	Derive 2 to 4 key results max. from your 3 to 5 objectives	• Team dialog objective and action area map	About 45 mins.
___:___	What exactly do we plan to do?	Derive measures with timing and responsibilities across the action areas and key results	• Team dialog objective and action area map • Flipchart	About 45 mins.
___:___	End			

Team: _____ Quarter: _____

Team quarterly objective derived from key results:

_____

_____

Key results:

_____

_____

Action areas:

_____

_____

"IT IS NOT THE STRONGEST OF THE SPECIES THAT SURVIVE, NOR THE MOST INTEL- LIGENT, BUT THE ONE MOST RESPONSIVE TO CHANGE."

Charles R. Darwin, British naturalist

TRANSFORM

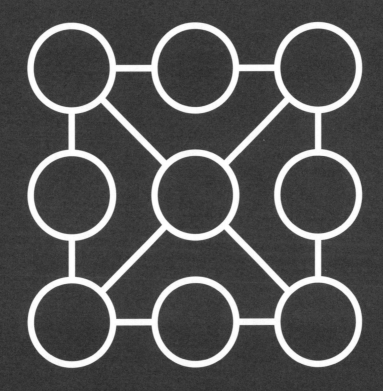

ACCELERATE CHANGE WITH A DUAL OPERATING SYSTEM

"The central issue is never strategy, structure, culture, or systems. The core of the matter is always about changing the behavior of people."
John P. Kotter, Professor of Leadership, Harvard Business School

The world we live, work and do business in today is often described as VUCA. Everything appears volatile, uncertain, complex, and ambiguous. We can no longer rely on our familiar toolset and the success factors of the past. The tried-and-trusted methods for implementing strategies that worked up to now are increasingly failing corporate executives amid stiff competition and sustained geopolitically driven deglobalization. It is becoming increasingly difficult to keep pace with the type and speed of change if you stay in reactive mode and let yourself be carried along by VUCA forces.

Traditional management processes are geared toward pre-defined decision hierarchies and set up to fulfil the daily requirements of a "normal" company business with operating routines effectively and efficiently. These processes seldom discover emerging dangers in time or recognize their potential dimension. They are not made for supplying strategic answers to unexpected threats, system changes or new opportunities, and molding them rapidly into strategic initiatives. The analyses of John Kotter (2012), the "supreme master" of change management, confirms that "a[ny] company that has made it past the start-up stage is optimized for efficiency rather than for strategic agility – the ability to capitalize on opportunities and dodge threats with speed and assurance."

That is a good enough reason for us to reshape the classic strategy cascade into an "agile" cascade with greater flexibility and maneuverability. We are therefore adopting the logic of quarterly achievement of objectives and key results from the OKR methodology to activate the entire organization in the existing hierarchy and order. But the work of the strategist does not end at this point with controlling the hierarchy cascade until the objective is achieved. Instead, the fun of strategy-making starts now!

BUILD AN INTERNAL STRATEGY NETWORK

The traditional implementation cascade is geared to the existing hierarchy and provides its contribution to achieving the set objectives across different hierarchical levels. But the transformation does not just move synchronously across all teams in the cascade at all, but at different speeds and intensities and in parallel asynchronous strands. You might even reform your organizational structure as one of the measures in the "Structures & Processes" action area. A reorganization like this generally triggers psychological uncertainty among those affected, which leads to reticence or even resistance and can reduce their contribution to achieving the objectives.

For that reason, Kotter (2014) recommends developing a "dual operating system". This means an internal community of decision-makers, multipliers, and supporters ("influencers") from different hierarchical levels and corporate areas who are strategically networked across the entire company. You might have already involved people like this in Strategy Workshop II. If not, it is high time to do so now. Make yourself more independent of your existing management cascade and the notorious "clay layer" of middle management. This will give you the necessary "reliability, efficiency, speed, and agility" to survive among the competition.

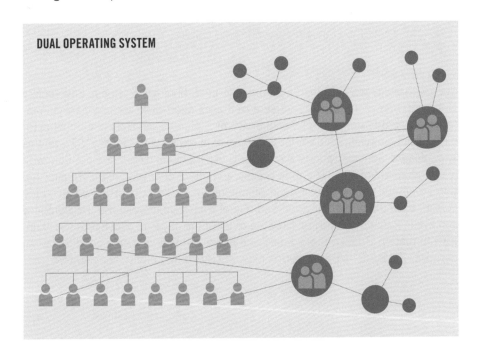

DUAL OPERATING SYSTEM

ACCELERATE THE CHANGE

Kotter (1996) introduced an eight-step model in his bestseller, *Leading Change,* that companies worldwide have adopted as the standard methodology for implementing change. The eight steps are:

1. Create a sense of urgency.
2. Form a leading coalition.
3. Develop a vision for change.
4. Communicate the vision, so that it will be supported by everyone.
5. Empowerment to broad-based actions.
6. Achieve short-term successes.
7. Never ease up.
8. Integrate the changes into corporate culture.

The massive, rapid, and disruptive change in technology, business and society is making hard-earned competitive advantages short-lived for companies. Yesterday's benefits (for example, economies of scale through size) can become today's disadvantages, as traditional commercial banks with "legacy" IT systems and bloated administrations are bitterly experiencing amid competition with lean and agile fintechs. The time pressure to effect change is high. Transformation processes can no longer be implemented at a calm, unhurried pace, as the current example of digitalization and digital transformation shows. No company can evade it. On the contrary. Now the order of the day is to accelerate the entire transformation. To take these heavily changed and still changing conditions into account, Kotter (2014) transforms his eight steps into eight "accelerators".

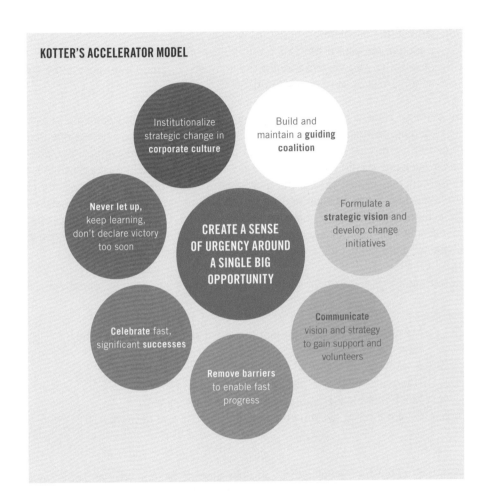

KOTTER'S ACCELERATOR MODEL

- Institutionalize strategic change in **corporate culture**
- Build and maintain a **guiding coalition**
- Never let up, keep learning, don't declare victory too soon
- **CREATE A SENSE OF URGENCY AROUND A SINGLE BIG OPPORTUNITY**
- Formulate a **strategic vision** and develop change initiatives
- **Celebrate** fast, significant **successes**
- **Communicate** vision and strategy to gain support and volunteers
- **Remove barriers** to enable fast progress

1. Instead of working through the eight steps sequentially and confined to themselves, the accelerators are simultaneously and continuously in action.

2. In Kotter's original model, the progress through the eight steps is propelled by a small core group. In the accelerator model, a strategic network alongside the management cascade ensures the involvement of as many people as possible from the entire organization.

3. The eight-step model is designed to be able to function within a traditional hierarchy, whereas the accelerator model relies on the flexibility and agility of a parallel, non-hierarchical network.

You can use the accelerator model for two key tasks:

(1) transforming your organization into a dual operating system and

(2) developing your organization at the company or group level across the six action areas of the StrategyFrame®.

In Strategy Workshop II you already decided which adaptions were necessary (for example, reorganizing the sales department, introducing a process-oriented organization, or changing the IT system and application landscape). Now, concrete measures should follow in accelerator mode. Who should be responsible for these concrete measures? On the one hand, it is the task and responsibility of the individual teams to align and integrate these measures with their measures for achieving the quarterly objective and key results. On the other hand, central management and control are required, as these types of measure have lighthouse character and radiate onto and pay into the entire transformation project.

Kotter highlights five critical success factors for achieving the acceleration:

1. Many change agents, not just the usual suspects, meaning the management executives.
2. A want-to and a get-to – not just a have-to – mindset.
3. Head and heart, not just head.
4. Much more leadership, not just more management.
5. Dual operating system comprising hierarchy and network.

With the help of the "accelerators" and the success factors, you can derive your concrete measures as well as the dramaturgy for the transformation, record them in the StrategyFrame® by updating the roadmap, and thus continuously push the transformation. We have simplified the accelerator package slightly to enable you to adapt the content and processes in your workflow.

STRATEGY ACCELERATORS

1. CONSTANTLY GENERATE A SENSE OF URGENCY AS TO YOUR TARGET VISION AND PARTICULARLY TO YOUR IMPACT STATEMENT.

It is critically important to convey the right appreciation of the transformation to your team. Urgency and desired impact must be expressed in the demeanor and attitude of corporate management and must be perceptible to every member of your organization every day. Naturally, there will have to be strategic adjustments in the course of the transformation. After all, the world will not stand still while you are transforming your company. However, you must never lose sight of the target vision when you make these adjustments.

The organization won't get moving without a suitable perspective. Hence you have to generate momentum. You have developed your strategy story from the challenges and impact statements described in your StrategyFrame®. It is the foundation for your transformation story which you will now announce in all media and at all public events. Bring your target vision and impact statements to life. Illustrate them from various perspectives. Be "loud". That's not your style? Make it your style. That is the only way you will be heard.

STORIES FROM THE FIELD

"Being loud" with its claim "Lead the Category" made innovative full-service electronics group KATEK successful. Born of the idea of consolidating the heavily fragmented market of small and medium-sized manufacturers of electronic assemblies with a "buy-and-build" story, this young company bravely set out to make European companies in all sectors less dependent on fragile global supply chains again as demanders of electronic components. After going public in 2021, all signs are pointing to market leadership: "Our branding, and particularly the claim, made the decisive difference for us. This enabled us to gain extraordinary talent and new companies for our group who wanted to be part of our success story," CEO Rainer Koppitz reported in our podcast.

2. BUILD A GUIDING COALITION AND MAINTAIN IT.

At the heart of the strategic network is a core group of volunteers from the entire organization, Kotter's "guiding coalition". Everyone can apply to be a member. There are no hierarchies. All members are on an equal footing and have access to the same information. This enables thought and action silos to be broken open and nests of resistance eliminated beyond all hierarchies.

In our experience, companies shy away from this type of procedure, especially in precarious situations or because the prevailing opinion is that too many cooks spoil the strategy broth. Then it is common practice to exclude the unruly spirits and eternal whiners. However, good strategy work integrates notorious critics sensibly and profitably too. Think about it and deliberate on who in your organization will fit into the transformation management team. To synchronize with the hierarchy cascade, we recommend that you expand the core team of your strategic network to include the management executives responsible for the five major objectives in the StrategyFrame®. Naturally, the top management level should be represented to the same extent as the manager responsible for the strategy process as coordinator.

3. GIVE THE NETWORK THE CAPACITY TO ELIMINATE ANY OBSTACLES THAT EMERGE OR SOLVE PROBLEMS.

STORIES FROM THE FIELD:

A large mechanical engineering company has an internal non-hierarchical strategic network that is meant to provide cross-divisional and cross-functional help with problem-solving and similar tasks. Network members get time credits when they are working as network members. Example: A product manager received a customer query with a totally new product requirement. Off the bat, the manager had neither an idea for a solution nor enough time to think about it appropriately, as the customer needed an answer as quickly as possible ("We have a problem. Can you solve it?"). So, the product manager asked the internal network for help. A network member with a free window of time got in touch: "I'll put together a team to solve the problem." The volunteer drafted a presentation and shared it in the network. Several colleagues with suitable professional and pertinent skills and a free window of time got in touch. The sender of the presentation took on the task of team leader to organize and coordinate the group. After a week, the group had found a pragmatic, software-based solution to the customer requirement. The customer was highly pleased with the speed of the company and the cost-effective solution.

How does that work in your organization? Would you be prepared to free up 20 percent of your resource capacity for network members?

4. DEVELOP A DRAMATURGY OF THE PROGRESS AND THE SUCCESSES. SHOWCASE THEM INDEPENDENTLY OF THE CURRENT STATUS OF DISCUSSIONS IN INDIVIDUAL INITIATIVES OR PROJECTS.

The credibility of the dual operating system depends to a large extent on whether it delivers visible and impactful results fast enough. Human patience is limited, especially among those who are in a state of psychological uncertainty and are afraid that they will be in the losing camp at the end of the transformation. The longer it takes, the easier it is for sceptics, whiners, and saboteurs to dilute achievements and erect obstacles. That is why you should celebrate milestones and all the successes that pay into your target vision. Use every type of communication on internal and external media to do this. Success inspires and emotionalizes. Take the people in your organization on board emotionally.

5. DON'T GIVE UP! CONTINUE TO LEARN FROM EXPERIENCES. DON'T DECLARE VICTORY TOO SOON.

You have to implement your strategic initiative within the action areas and constantly create new ones to adapt to a changing business environment and stay competitive. If you take your foot off the gas, the process loses its momentum and gives resistance lots of space to develop.

That is the crucial reason why the situation analysis and its accompanying challenges are so central to the urgency of your strategy process. The only thing that keeps people moving is what is important and simultaneously urgent. If the urgency is too weak at the beginning or is neglected, the determination in the strategic network swiftly declines and the focus shifts back to the hierarchy.

6. INSTITUTIONALIZE STRATEGIC CHANGES IN YOUR ORGANIZATION'S CULTURE.

Strategic initiatives have not been completed until they have been transferred and integrated into daily routines. For that reason, you should not just embed factual results from the gradual execution of the defined work packages. Every initiative brings new requirements and challenges for the thoughts and actions of the participants. Shared learning and retraining as well as sharing the learnings with others in the organization generate new organizational knowledge that can be used creatively and innovatively for the company's competitiveness. Continuous strategic learning (Pietersen, 2001) will change your organization and create a culture of openness to new things, agility in thoughts and actions, and sustainability of action.

TRANSFORM

To implement your strategy, you must now transform your entire organization one step at a time. You have already laid the foundation for this in all action areas in the "Adapt" process step, and more important measures were added on the various team levels in your company in "Cascade". Now set the transformation in motion with the six strategy accelerators and get it up to the required speed.

KEY QUESTIONS:

1. How should we start the transformation to generate lasting change?

2. How will we overcome obstacles and resistance in the existing hierarchy?

3. Who will be members of the transformation steering committee – the core transformation team?

4. How will we activate previously unused powers within the entire organization and shape these into a strategic network?

5. How will we create the necessary communication infrastructure and content to accelerate the journey?

6. How can we establish strong symbols for the urgency of change as well as for our impact statement?

7. How will we embed the systemic changes into structures and processes?

8. How will we inspire the people in the organization and incite them to actively join us on the journey?

INSTRUCTIONS

1. Start the application and selection process for the strategy community and the transformation steering committee.
2. Decide on dates for the inaugural meeting of the steering committee as well as for the meeting and reporting routine.
3. Ensure synchronization with the strategy cascade and its routines.
4. Launch the strategy network with clear rules of play and with your backing.
5. Develop a viable, multidirectional infrastructure and content structure for your communication and the interaction within the network.
6. Develop an exciting dramaturgy along the change curve to showcase successes and to inspire.

TIPS

Appointment recommendations for the guiding coalition (transformation steering committee):
• Sponsor of the strategy process
• Strategy process manager
• Sponsor of the five objectives
• Five representatives from the strategic network from all hierarchical levels and corporate areas (if possible also diverse with regard to gender, age, nationality, ...)
Restrict the group to 12 members, as otherwise the dynamism will be lost because of the size of the group.

Appointment to the strategic network: Combine suggestions from the existing hierarchy with an open internal application process that includes a motivational letter or video. When you are appointing the network members, make sure you cover all regional, functional, and operational areas of your company.

CAUTION

Experience shows that it is generally the good, popular (agreeable) and willing employees who are proposed for important working groups or pilot projects. But time is the scarcest of all resources. Generally, these usual suspects are already excessively busy with day-to-day business and in other projects along the strategy cascade. You must therefore give the network sufficient time resources and relieve them of other tasks. Your networkers should be able to use at least 20 to 40 percent of their work time for the transformation. Alongside suggestions, you should also let the colleagues' initiative decide.

TRANSFORMATION STEERING COMMITTEE

MEMBERS:

Strategy sponsor: _____

Strategy process manager: _____

Sponsor objective 1: _____   Community 1: _____

Sponsor objective 2: _____   Community 2: _____

Sponsor objective 3: _____   Community 3: _____

Sponsor objective 4: _____   Community 4: _____

Sponsor objective 5: _____   Community 5: _____

Strategy cascade update routine:

Frequency: _____   Data: ___.___._____

Kickoff transformation steering committee: ___.___._____   Meeting frequency: _____

Strategy cascade tracking tool: _____

Transformation program tracking tool: _____

STRATEGIC COMMUNITY

Start of the application process: ___.___._____

Selection criteria: _____

Nomination procedure: _____

Number of members at the start of the community (to cover all locations): _____

INFRASTRUCTURE FOR COMMUNICATION & COOPERATION

CHANNELS	URGENCY & IMPACT STATEMENTS	PROCESS & SUCCESS REPORTS	COMMUNITY INTERACTION	STEERING COMMITTEE INTERACTION	BACKGROUND STORIES & STRATEGIC CLASSIFICATION
E.g., Teams channel community			✓		

ROADMAP III

AREA

TRANSFORMATION DRAMATURGY

MONTH/QUARTER

PHASES

MILESTONES

MEASURES

**EMOTIONAL
REACTION –**
Change curve adapted from
Kübler-Ross (1969)

1. PREMONITION
WORRY

2. SHOCK
FRIGHT

3. RESISTANCE
ANGER

REALIZATION

PRODUCTIVY GAIN

PRODUCTIVY LOss

7. INTEGRATION
SELF-CONFIDENCE

5. EMOTIONAL ACCEPTANCE
SADNESS

6. OPENNESS
**CURIOSITY,
ENTHUSIASM**

4. RATIONAL ACCEPTANCE
FRUSTRATION

TIME

"THE REASON WHY IT IS SO DIFFICULT FOR EXISTING FIRMS TO CAPITALIZE ON DISRUPTIVE INNOVATIONS IS THAT THEIR PROCESSES AND THEIR BUSINESS MODEL THAT MAKE THEM GOOD AT THE EXISTING BUSINESS ACTUALLY MAKE THEM BAD AT COMPETING FOR THE DISRUPTION."

Clayton M. Christensen, US economist, author, and management consultant

EXPERIMENT

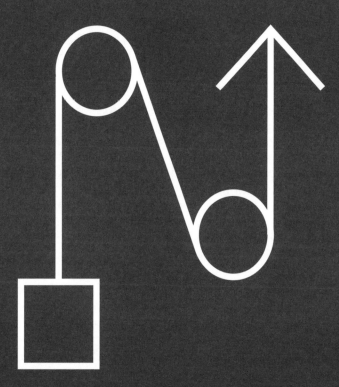

GROWTH ENGINE FOR THE DAY AFTER TOMORROW

"Experimentation can be defined as an iterative process of learning, what does and does not work. The goal of a business experiment is actually not a product or solution; it is learning – the kind of learning about customers, markets, and possible options that will lead you to the right solution."
David L. Rogers, consultant, author and faculty member for Digital Strategy & Marketing, Columbia Business School.

You are using the current strategy process to reorient your company with an eye to the future. You want to maximize competitiveness and resilience. But strategy execution is still an experiment. On the one hand, your strategy will contain new elements and you do not know yet today how they will function internally or for the customer tomorrow. On the other hand, you are not rolling out your strategy in a vacuum, but under competitive pressure in an environment that is constantly changing.

For example, if your strategy envisages a more aggressive price and sales policy to increase your share in a particular market, you will be attacking your competitors directly. They could then react aggressively and lower their prices to defend their market position. Lower prices please the customers but reduce corporate profits. But your competitors could also fight back in a different market where you are reliant on a higher price level for profitability reasons. Therefore, when you transform, do not just hope for the best, as the title of our book suggests, presuming that, "It will all work out".

Your company – like us all – is a part of diverse systems that overlap and compete from the micro to the macro level. Therefore, your activities do not just produce results where you would like, they can also lead to unexpected consequences in other parts of a system. That is why it is important to identify systemic interactions between your strategy elements, understand their nature and assess their implications. You can reduce your implementation risk by testing out critical strategy elements (for instance, new price offers) gradually and iteratively (for example, in different, clearly demarcated test markets).

If the experimentation is successful, is that as good as it gets? Of course not, because the old footballer's adage applies: There is always a next game. The next disruption could already lie in wait at the next trade fair or come from the next start-up. So, continue your thought process: Which capabilities and resources are already in your company that you could use to develop the growth engine for the day after tomorrow. Now you might retort: "Yes, that is all well and good, but just let us finish up the current strategy process first."

Yes, you should always finish what you started, but in case you have not noticed yet, there is no end to the process when you make it your new strategic routine.

And in this routine of constantly reviewing and adjusting, the question about the growth engine for the day after tomorrow will automatically come up. Irrespective of where the next disruption comes from or what forces are driving it, the best way to be prepared, conquer your challenges and dominate new growth areas is, according to Anthony et al. (2017), a "dual transformation":

"Dual transformation is the greatest challenge a leadership team will ever face. It is also the greatest opportunity a leadership team will encounter."

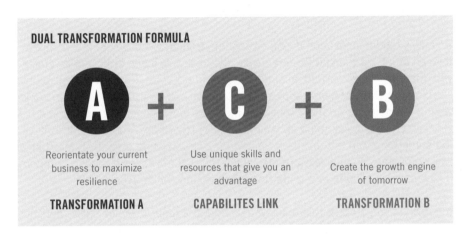

The A stands for the strategy process that you are currently going through. Of course, there are sufficient topics in this process that you can test gradually and sparingly before or during the implementation. Experimentation promotes learning. And if you want to still be relevant and successful the day after tomorrow, you should consider that you might have to generate your future growth outside the core business depicted in A. If you have already decided on one of the three strategic courses of action

- Identification of value offerings
- Market identification
- Future diversification

in the target vision when you were determining the playing field, you will find the instructions for developing it here.

CREATE THE GROWTH ENGINE = B

Searching for new markets, new demand and new business models is a major strategic challenge that you have to face with farsightedness, openness in your thought processes and agility in your actions. Overcoming this challenge generally requires new resources and skills as well as a different approach compared to your established markets. In addition, the future field of activity can look completely different to the current one. For this reason, we have uncoupled the duality process step from reorienting core business in A in the first run.

Business model innovation is one option for strategically developing a company. Instead of letting yourself be "creatively destroyed" or made irrelevant by others, you "destroy" your current business model in good time and establish a new one. Real-world experience shows that "creative self-destruction" seldom works when "the house is on fire", your core business is no longer watertight, and the strategy crisis is consuming all your energy. Furthermore, it is difficult to develop something new within the boundaries of the existing organization. That is why companies frequently split off exploratory initiatives from regular company business into independent units (for example, innovation labs).

If you want to go down this road, you will need a team that has skills, horizons of experience and personalities that will be able to not just think "out of our own box" but "beyond the boxes". This means having strategic foresight as well as understanding trends and developments on the macro and micro levels. If you want to build your future growth engine, you will need investments and stable financial resources. And no one knows whether anything usable will come out of the future lab. There are no guarantees, but a multitude of risks. That means that you will have to convince those in your company who tend to prefer lower risk about the search for the future engine and the rationale of the associated use of scarce resources.

HOW DO YOU FIND YOUR B?

New business models are usually born when new business opportunities are recognized in a market on the supply or demand side. The founders of Netflix cancelled out Blockbusters' stationary movie lending business when they recognized that the new DVD technology was ideally suited for mailing. Additionally, Amazon provided them with a functioning model for mail order. The combination of new technology and new sales approach created a new business model. Similarly, the business models used by Uber, Airbnb and other digital intermediaries are based on the realization that supply and demand can be coordinated better and profitably, or even created from scratch, with the help of technology.

How should you proceed? You have to identify problems, weaknesses or defects in your potential focus markets which have not been addressed, or not adequately addressed, up to now because specialized skills were lacking, potential solutions are too expensive or inconvenient under current conditions or customers cannot yet imagine better solutions. Your first task now is to find better, cheaper or more convenient solutions. After that, you will develop a business model that overcomes existing barriers, serves the market profitably and can ensure your future. Examine the various options for getting your new business model to the starting line, for example, the establishment of a new company, a spin-off from the current company, acquisitions or participations in established companies or startups.

DISCOVER UNIQUE CAPABILITIES = C

This is truly the most difficult part of the dual journey. What skills and resources does your company need to be relevant and successful in the future? Which unique capabilities and growth potential lie dormant in your company? Essentially, this is about building the bridge from the existing skills and resources, as well as those that must be developed, from your current company to the growth leader of tomorrow. That is the "capabilities link".

Take a step back: Which skills and resources define your current corporate competencies? To what extent are they determined by your brand and the knowledge that has accumulated within your company?

The future is not a linear continuation of the present. That is why you have to be aware that your current core competencies probably won't pay into your growth initiatives for the future.

Encourage your teams to think about core competencies and growth potential and exchange ideas about them with each other. Ensure that sufficient time, personnel and financial resources are set aside for B and C. Visibly dedicate your personal attention and support to this part of the dual transformation. Anthony et al. (2017) summarize your challenge concisely:

"Creating a new business from scratch is hard, but executives of incumbents have the dual challenge of creating new businesses while simultaneously staving off never-ending attacks on existing operations, which provide vital cash flow and capabilities to invest in growth."

What now? We have not answered one key question up to now: How do you find these unique skills and resources that generate growth potential and inspire new business models for tomorrow and the day after tomorrow?

GENERATE IDEAS WITH STRATEGIC INTUITION

"A good hockey player plays where the puck is. A great hockey player plays where the puck is going to be."
Wayne Gretzky, former Canadian ice hockey player

How do your new ideas develop? And how do your ideas develop into business models? Are thinking headspace and inspiration enough to create something groundbreaking new for your company?

To Joseph Schumpeter (1911), innovation was primarily creating the new by combining the old in a new way. And the old does not necessarily have to come from within your company. On the contrary:

"Good artists copy – great artists steal."
Steve Jobs, former US entrepreneur, founder and CEO of Apple Inc.

This witticism that Steve Jobs ascribed to artist Pablo Picasso stands for the capability of the Apple co-founder to think outside of their own box, to help themselves to the good and successful things that are already there, but see them in a new way and combine them with their own ideas in such a way that something new emerged. Let us take Apple's iPod and iPhone as examples. The analog precursor to the iPod was the Sony Walkman, the first portable miniature cassette recorder. Steve Jobs "digitalized" the Walkman. In the case of the iPhone, he made the cell phone "smart". In both cases, only a few wheels had to be completely reinvented. Jobs "borrowed" the design of the iPod and iPhone from German industrial designer Dieter Rams and his work for electrical appliance manufacturer Braun, including the T3 transistor radio (1958) or the ET66 pocket calculator (1987).

Ideas come before innovation. When do you get your best ideas? Probably during the night or in the shower, or in a totally unexpected moment. Suddenly it hits you – you have a flash of inspiration. In your mind's eye, things fit together that you had never associated with one another before. Thoughts combine and manifest themselves as an idea.

Brain research has examined how these flashes of inspiration arise. It is a particular form of intuition. There are three types of intuition. Regular intuition can best be understood as our "gut feeling". It arises from experiences, knowledge and projections. Specialist intuition constitutes the quick judgements we make because we perceive something familiar or analog and basically know the consequences. In such decision-making situations, we are "experts" and our brain generates an expert assessment. Just like experienced footballers can deduce where a ball will go from the way and the speed a ball is played. The third type of intuition is more than just a gut or expert feeling. Instead, it gives us an idea for our future action. That is why Duggan (2007) called this type of intuition "strategic intuition".

Strategic intuition is a clear thought. And it is not quick like expert intuition. It is slow. The flash of inspiration you had yesterday evening could solve a problem that may have occupied your mind for quite some time already. And it does not in familiar situations, like in a football game. Strategic intuition functions in new or different situations, when the gut and expert feelings provide no solutions. That is when we need strategic intuition the most.

Carl von Clausewitz, a Prussian general in the Napoleonic Wars and trailblazer of modern strategy theory, analyzed Napoleon's successes on the battlefield. He discovered that Napoleon had particularly strong strategic intuition. Clausewitz defined strategic intuition as a four-step process. On the first step, you need "historical awareness". Napoleon had carefully studied past battles, learned from them and used the insights for his own battles. Thus, today's strategists should be familiar with what has happened up to now or is already available. Steve Jobs was a fan of the Bauhaus design school and Dieter Rams' work.

But knowledge and familiarity alone are not enough. On the second step, you have to add presence of mind. When Steve Jobs visited Xerox Labs in the early 1970s, he saw a minicomputer in the research lab with a graphic user interface that could be controlled by a device that we call a mouse nowadays. His alert mind combined what he had seen with his own vision: the Apple personal computer. The flash of inspiration, the third step in strategic intuition, ignited and supplied the idea for action. And to get into action, the last step you need in strategic intuition is decisiveness. Steve Jobs had the necessary decisiveness: from Apple I (1976) to today's notebook.

You can use Duggan's (2013) "Insight Matrix", which was developed in collaboration with General Electric, for your idea generation process. It captures problem solutions or their achievement elements from other areas (companies, sectors, markets) or contexts (sport, theater, …). The aim is to combine the various elements in such a way that new solutions emerge. The following matrix shows the example of Netflix.

	PROBLEM 1					PROBLEM 2	

PROBLEM 1
DVD rental club online orders

PROBLEM 2
Online Streaming

SOURCES

ELEMENTS	BLOCK-BUSTER	FITNESS CLUB	AMAZON	DVDS	OTHERS?	AWS CLOUD	NAPSTER
TYPE OF BUSINESS	✓		✓				
PAYMENT SYSTEM		✓	✓				
DELIVERY SYSTEM			✓		✓		
ONLINE SERVER						✓	
ON-DEMAND STREAMING							✓

INSIGHT MATRIX
NETFLIX I + II extended according
to Duggan (2013)

STORIES FROM THE FIELD

Netflix combined the new DVD technology with the digital sales model it adopted from Amazon into a completely new business model. In addition, the company ensured it always had the biggest possible inventory of movies on DVD. The advantages were obvious. With Netflix, customers could select from a huge stock of movies, simply order the desired movies over the internet and have them delivered to their homes. They had no time or travel costs to get to the next video store. Netflix saved on the fixed store and personnel costs of stationary business operations. Later, Netflix immediately adapted new technological developments from the IT area, especially the cloud offerings from Amazon Web Services (AWS), and exited the DVD mail order model to establish a new business model: "video on demand" via "internet streaming". Customers no longer had to wait for the delivery to arrive.

The relationship between Netflix and AWS is an example of collaboration with simultaneous competition, known in business jargon as "co-opetition". AWS earns from every Netflix user's "stream" and at the same time offers a direct competitor product, Amazon Prime. On the one side of the business model, AWS and Netflix are collaborating, while on the other side, the competition for every subscription is fierce.

ESTABLISH A STRATEGIC INNOVATION ROUTINE

Don't leave the detection of new market or business opportunities to chance. Integrate that too into your day-after-tomorrow-focused thought process in your strategy process for tomorrow. Set up a work routine that comprises the following steps:

1. IDENTIFY THE PROBLEM

Let us assume you are looking at a focus market. Start by writing down with your team the current understanding of the market conditions and customer benefit. Identify the potential problems or opportunities on the supply and demand side that are related to customer benefit. Who are your current customers? Who could your future customers be? Compile personas of your current and future customers. Personas are models of "typical" customers or users that characterize people in a target group according to their features. Which value propositions would they find appealing? Which offering elements (price, quality and the like) generate the main benefit for your personas? Collect these elements in the insight matrix.

2. FIND SUCCESSFUL MODELS

Look at your trend radar in the process step "Analyze"

Search for potential solutions or models of solutions in other areas or contexts. Enter these models into your insight matrix. Use the situation analysis in the "Trends" module of the StrategyFrame®as inspiration for your search. Which macrotrends are impacting on your sector and your business model? Which microtrends are relevant for your personas?

3. COMBINE THE MODELS INTO NEW SOLUTIONS

Combining the various solution elements from different sources is a creative process: Which elements fit together, which need to be modified or added to achieve a bigger customer benefit profitably? Which elements can be dispensed with?

Create the best possible conditions for strategic intuition. Creativity does not work on demand just because you have a design thinking workshop today. Give your team members time for a homework assignment: to develop promising solutions independently. The list of solution proposals will then be the input for the team workshop where the proposals are presented and discussed individually. Then decide together with your team which proposals should be pursued further. Present this shortened list to an extended circle of management executives and specialist executives.

Keep an open mind for suggestions or even new ideas. At the end, select the top 3 solutions that should go into the next phase together.

4. CREATE NEW VALUE PROPOSITIONS AND DEVELOP NEW BUSINESS MODEL PROTOTYPES

Elaborate the specific benefit or value propositions to your personas for your top 3 solutions. Starting with these value propositions you can develop prototypes for potential business models with the aid of the familiar "Business Model Canvas".

BUSINESS MODEL CANVAS & VALUE PROPOSITION adapted according to Osterwalder (2010)

KEY PARTNERS	KEY ACTIVITIES	VALUE PROPOSITIONS	CUSTOMER RELATIONSHIPS	CUSTOMER SEGMENTS
Who are your most important partners for achieving competitive advantages?	What are the most important steps for getting closer to your customers?	How will you make your customers' lives happier?	How often will you contact your customers?	Who are your customers?
	KEY RESOURCES Which resources do you need to realize your idea?	**PRODUCTS AND SERVICES** **PROFIT GENERATORS** **PROBLEM SOLVERS**	**CHANNELS** How do you want to reach your customers?	**CUSTOMER JOBS** **PROFITS** **PAIN POINTS**

COST STRUCTURE	REVENUE STREAMS
How much are you planning for product development and marketing in a certain time period?	• How much are you planning for? • How much do you want to earn in a certain time period? • Compare your costs and income.

Alexander Osterwalder, inventor of the Business Model Canvas, summarizes this as follows:

"Once you understand business models you can then start prototyping business models just like you prototype products."

The Canvas comprises the core elements required for the creation and profitability of your value proposition. You must answer the following questions for every business model prototype:

- Which resources and skills will we have to use for a cost-effective value proposition?
- Which activities are required for it? Do we need partners for it? If so, which ones?
- Who are our target customers (customer groups)?
- Which channels will we use to reach our target customers?
- What relationships do we need to build with our target customers to continuously generate sufficiently high revenues to achieve our profitability objectives?

Answering these questions will also help you to understand which of your current skills or resources are not so easy for your competition to copy and could additionally create potential benefits for the growth engine for the day after tomorrow.

5. TEST AND LEARN

"Your No. 1 goal is to reduce the risk of failure and uncertainty."
Alexander Osterwalder, Swiss author and inventor of the Business Model Canvas

Test your business model prototypes on potential customers. That will enable you to reduce the risk of developing something that no one really needs or will buy. Learn from the feedback from your test customers. Continue to adapt the prototypes until you find a model that justifies the investment and development up to market maturity. Consider well which path you want to go down in the market (go-to-market). Will that work with your existing company, or will you gain market access, for example, through acquisitions?

When you are experimenting, don't forget: Strategy is a plan. It has to be flexible to be able to adapt to the constantly changing conditions in your market, the competition, in trends and in your broader environment.

"THE MORE SYSTEMATICALLY PEOPLE ACT, THE MORE EFFECTIVELY WILL CHANCE HIT THEM."

Friedrich Dürrenmatt, Swiss author, dramatist, and artist

EXPERIMENT

Constantly reinventing yourself and never standing still has become a requirement of our fast-moving times. That means you must put strategy innovation work into your company routine. To kick off, we suggest holding a two-day workshop with a diverse team from across your organization to present the new routine and your methods and subsequently transport them into your company. One thing is important: Define and communicate a clear process for how new ideas should develop and from them real new business so that the new routine does not turn into worthless "busy work".

KEY QUESTIONS:

1. Which unique skills and resources do you have in your core business that could create an advantage for you for tomorrow and maybe even the day after tomorrow?

2. Which trends are changing your sector and threatening your business model?

3. Which problem will you have to solve for your customers tomorrow?

4. Are there models of successful problem solutions in other environments or contexts already?

5. How can these models be combined into new solutions for your potential customers and their problems?

6. Which value propositions could you make to your personas with these new solution combinations?

7. What does your potential business model look like for each value proposition?
   Which unique skills and resources can you build on for this?

8. How will you test your prototypes to reduce risks as much as possible?

9. What could your growth engine of tomorrow look like?

INSTRUCTIONS
(You will find the detailed description on the previous pages.)

1. Identify the problem.
2. Find successful models.
3. Combine the models into new solutions.
4. Create new value propositions and develop new business model prototypes.
5. Test and learn.

INSIGHT MATRIX

PROBLEM

SOURCES

ELEMENTS							

BUSINESS MODEL CANVAS according to Osterwalder (2010)

KEY PARTNERS	KEY ACTIVITIES	VALUE PROPOSITIONS	CUSTOMER RELATIONSHIPS	CUSTOMER SEGMENTS
	KEY ACTIVITIES		**CHANNELS**	

COST STRUCTURE	REVENUE STREAMS

"IF YOU INTEND TO RENEW YOURSELF, DO IT EVERY DAY."

Confucius

ADJUST

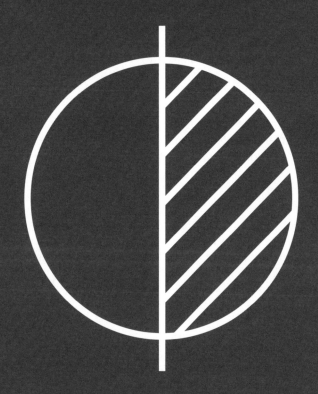

CONTINUOUSLY ADJUST YOUR COURSE

"Dangers await only those who do not react to life. He who picks up the stimuli emanating from society and designs his policy accordingly does not need to fear difficulties."

Mikhail S. Gorbachev, last President of the Soviet Union.

Shutdowns of cities and ports due to COVID-19, exploding energy prices, suspension of gas deliveries for your industry, acute water shortages at production sites, uncertainty among consumers who are restricting their consumption because of inflation fears, a new conflict between China and Taiwan – it feels like the world is turning faster than ever before. Events that were once far away and of no significance to your company – they don't exist anymore. Everything is connected. Today, you should probably find it interesting to know if the proverbial sack of rice falls over in China.

Amid the most recent geopolitical and pandemic developments, international interdependencies and the globality of supply chains are changing radically and unpredictably. So how flexible does your strategy have to be? How often should you adjust your strategy? Every three years, once a year, once a quarter, monthly, or ad hoc?

The final process step in our strategy workflow is the continuous adjustment of the strategy you are implementing. For many companies, this constitutes the greatest challenge. But at the same time there is also great scope for misunderstandings here. What do we need to adjust within which time frames? And if we have to be constantly adjusting, isn't developing a strategy a waste of time anyway?

The answer is: No. There are elements, like, for example, your target vision, that you should keep firmly in your sights. But you have to constantly check the path you are on to reach it and adjust course in the event of large stumbling blocks, wrong equipment, or unexpected changes in terrain. Likewise, if your initial situation changes, you should clarify whether you are still on course and will be able to reach your target vision within the desired time frame.

If demand shifts in your markets or a competitor launches a major encroachment, you have to examine what that means for you. Naturally, you will not do that every week, unless the occurrence is so incisive that it requires a speedy risk assessment. Furthermore, you will not change your target vision with its associated impact statement, customer benefit and playing field within a year either. A considerably longer half-life should be applied to the impact statement and customer benefit. However, this could be different for your objectives and key results. Here you can fine-tune and reprioritize easily, for example, to keep your organization agile. You will have different time frames in the action areas for initiatives, projects and measures, as well as for their expansion and amendment. On the one hand, you should adjust the associated roadmap at least monthly to stay on track. On the other hand, you should only put the entire StrategyFrame® under the microscope once a year.

STEP BY STEP

A new strategy is an incisive experience for every company. Its implementation entails a lot of changes. Some of them might be small steps, others more evolutionary and others again absolutely system-altering and therefore revolutionary. We hope we have given you many stimuli and recommendations for your strategy process in this book. These suggestions won't always meet with approval in your organization – despite the involvement and participation of those affected – because they call experienced realities, traditions or simply habits into question. You are very ambitious to be taking on a new strategy. To make sure you don't overextend yourself, you should also examine yourself and regularly question your own thoughts and actions. Big changes always start with little ones. Take it step by step – to be a little better every day.

ESTABLISH NEW STRATEGY ROUTINES

"Can one tiny change transform your life? (...) The holy grail of habit change is not a single 1 percent improvement, but a thousand of them. It's a bunch of atomic habits stacking up, each one a fundamental unit of the overall system. (...) Each improvement is like adding a grain of sand to the positive side of the scale, slowly tilting things in your favor."

From the perspective of people successfully changing behavior, Clear (2020) describes how tiny changes can have a big impact. And after all, despite all the rationality and earnestness, there is also a lot of humanity inherent in your strategy process. Nothing in this process is really possible without the ideas, the commitment and the persistence that you, your management team and everyone in your organization put in.

Transform your new habits into routines with the StrategyFrame®.

STRATEGY ROUTINES

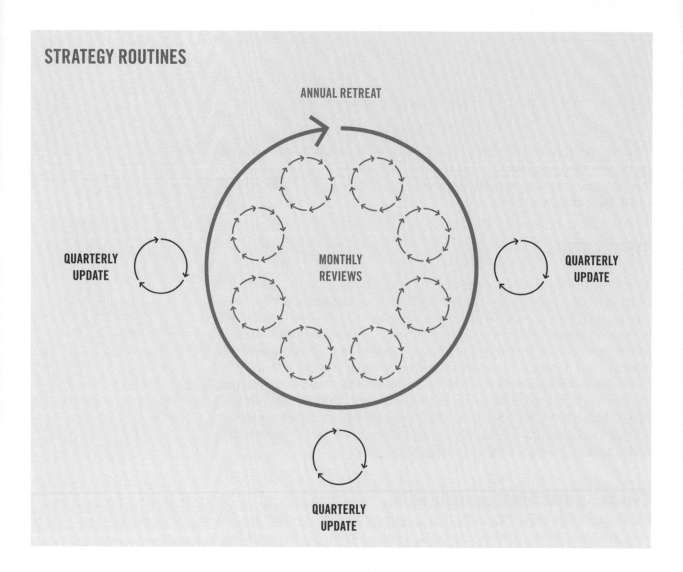

ANNUAL RETREAT

QUARTERLY UPDATE

MONTHLY REVIEWS

QUARTERLY UPDATE

QUARTERLY UPDATE

ROUTINE OVERVIEW

SYMBOL	CYCLE	MEETING FORMAT	DURATION	STRATEGYFRAME® MODULE
	3 to 5 years	Strategy Workshops I-III	see Process steps 1–4	Entire module
	1 x per year	Strategy Retreat	2 days	Situation analysis (markets, customer segments, offering, objectives & key results)/target vision (objectives & key results)/action areas (roadmap)
	3 x per year	Strategy Update	1 day	Situation analysis (market, competition, trends, broader environment)/target vision (objectives & key results)/action areas (innovation, roadmap)
	8 x per year	Strategy Review	0.5 day	Target vision (objectives & key results)/action areas (innovation, roadmap)
	If urgently needed	Strategy Check	tbd.	Situation analysis (unusual events arising from competitor environment, broader environment)/action areas (structures & processes, people, culture, data & IT)

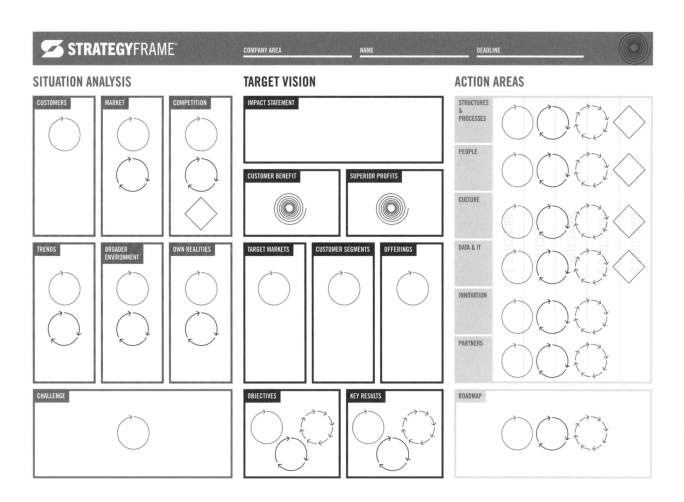

SITUATION ANALYSIS

CUSTOMERS MARKET COMPETITION

TRENDS BROADER ENVIRONMENT OWN REALITIES

CHALLENGE

TARGET VISION

IMPACT STATEMENT

CUSTOMER BENEFIT SUPERIOR PROFITS

TARGET MARKETS CUSTOMER SEGMENTS OFFERINGS

OBJECTIVES KEY RESULTS

ACTION AREAS

STRUCTURES & PROCESSES

PEOPLE

CULTURE

DATA & IT

INNOVATION

PARTNERS

ROADMAP

ROUTINES AFTER WORKFLOW & COMMITTEES

	STRATEGY SPONSOR + MANAGEMENT + PROCESS MANAGER	OBJECTIVES SPONSORS (MAX. 5 PEOPLE)	COMMUNITY REPRESENTATIVES (MAX. 5 PEOPLE)	INNOVATION MANAGERS (MAX. 10 PEOPLE)
OBJECTIVES COMMITTEE	✓	✓		
TRANSFORMATION STEERING COMMITTEE	✓	✓	✓	
INNOVATION STEERING COMMITTEE	✓			✓

CASCADE   TRANSFORM   EXPERIMENT   **ADJUST**   265

MEETING ROUTINES

STRATEGY CHECK

An ad-hoc format at the level of the steering committees that only comes into play if far-reaching and incisive events or changes occur in the markets or the broader environment. When there are general obstacles in strategy implementation at the operational level, the format provides an opportunity to develop solutions quickly on site without going through big committees.

STRATEGY REVIEW

A monthly format to examine the teams' progress as well as to check the achievement of the objectives and key results in the "Objectives" steering committee. The task of the "Transformation" steering committee (comprising five representatives from the "Objectives" as well as representatives from the strategy network) comprises the progress check, any resource issues and risks regarding the implementation of initiatives, projects and measures in the action areas as well as adjustments to the roadmap, if these are necessary.

STRATEGY UPDATE

A quarterly format to bring all group levels and steering committees up to speed on the areas of market, competitors and broader environment and discuss adjustment options.

The "Objectives" steering committee compares the objectives and key results, specifies new ones for the next quarter and cascades these down in the existing hierarchy.

The "Transformation" steering committee discusses the distribution of resources, the risk assessment as well as the approval of further far-reaching measures and updates the roadmap.

The "Innovation" steering committee evaluates the relevant microtrends based on the current trend radar and decides on the action required. It also examines the current status of ongoing innovation measures and approves new funding for tests. Preparation for innovation projects in another status or the implementation of venture capital projects are also discussed here.

STRATEGY RETREAT

Once a year, you should set aside 2 days with your management team to question all the major elements of your StrategyFrame®. Based on a comprehensively updated situation analysis, you will examine which challenges exist, how far you have come in creating your playing field, if your measures are working and paying into the achievement of the target vision and where your innovation projects stand. You can conduct the "target-actual" comparison on all important levels and fine-tune if necessary.

ADJUST

Your environment is not standing still. At the same time, your company is moving in the direction defined by the new strategy. This means constant adjustment – not of the whole thing, but of many small parameters so that you can consistently stay on the strategy implementation track.

KEY QUESTIONS:

1. Are your markets changing, is there any news about the competition, or are there far-reaching events pending in the broader environment that were not foreseeable? Who is responsible for the updates, or can these be automated?

2. Are there new trends for which urgent action is required?

3. How often should you adjust your strategy and the individual modules in the StrategyFrame®?

4. How is your objective achievement progressing? What is hindering this, or can you up the ante?

5. Who is serving on which steering committees?

6. Who ensures the synchronization of the overall process and the individual committees?

7. When should you launch a completely new strategy process?

INSTRUCTIONS

1. Define the various steering committees for 6 to 12 months in advance.
2. Ensure that the coordinating committees at team or community level are also stipulated for 6 to 12 months.
3. Appoint the participants of the individual committees as well as a chairperson for each one.
4. Ensure the availability of a clear and centrally accessible tracking system.
5. Define managers, service providers and/or tools for the updates in the module "Market", for "Competition", for "Broader Environment" and "Trends".
6. Determine when you want to launch the next full-fledged strategy process.

TIP

Use the StrategyFrame® and the associated cards for the individual modules to conduct the adjustment. This ensures that the old data is retained, and and you still have an overview of the overall context of the individual components that are changing.

CAUTION

Ensure that information about adjusted objectives and measures is communicated across the horizontal and vertical axes. With the passage of time, individual colleagues frequently succumb to the temptation to disappear into their silos again or no longer adhere to the collective agreements. Then there is a risk not only that the implementation will come to a standstill, but also of a potential asynchronicity in your strategy implementation as well as in your business model.

SET STRATEGY ROUTINES

	STRATEGY REVIEW	STRATEGY UPDATE	MANAGER	PARTICIPANTS
OBJECTIVES STEERING COMMITTEE				7
TRANSFORMATION STEERING COMMITTEE				12
INNOVA-TION STEERING COMMITTEE				Tbd.
TEAM COORDINATION				
COMMUNITY UPDATE				
INNOVATION TEAMS				

UPDATE Manager/Service provider/Tools:

Market: _____
_____

Competition: _____
_____

Broader environment: _____
_____

Trends: _____
_____

Start new strategy process ____.____._____

THE DIGITAL STRATEGYFRAME®

SOFTWARE, PLATFORM & COMMUNITY

STRATEGY-FRAME.COM

Above and beyond our book, we want to support you as best we can in developing and implementing your strategy with your team autonomously. Gone are the days of PowerPoint battles and Excel marathons when management executives and company owners could hammer out the new corporate strategy successfully behind closed doors. The book gave us the idea for a new strategy software to support you along the entire strategy workflow, through the individual process steps, tasks, meeting formats and your work with the StrategyFrame®.

Our digital solution offers you a central strategy platform for your team for the first time: strategy end-to-end, from planning through data collection, analyses, and workshop design right up to living your new strategy routines and success monitoring. Strategy in digital format – simple use, powerful outcome.

STRATEGY AS A SERVICE

In addition, we have assembled smart packages for your personal support which you can book for a fixed price for using the digital StrategyFrame®. Would you like to transfer the management and coordination of your strategy process across the entire workflow to an external and neutral person for reasons of internal politics or efficiency considerations? Do you need a moderator for a workshop? Or when the work is done, do you just need a formulation check for your communication? Our certified and experienced Strategy Makers are at your service for these and other tasks.

You too can profit from our selected digital partner offers, for example, for data collection, market or trend analyses. You can book these additional services directly from the digital workflow.

Using the code on page 9, you will receive a 10 percent discount on our user licenses as a reader of this book.

We look forward to welcoming you to our Strategy Maker community with its many benefits and all the latest from the world of strategy.

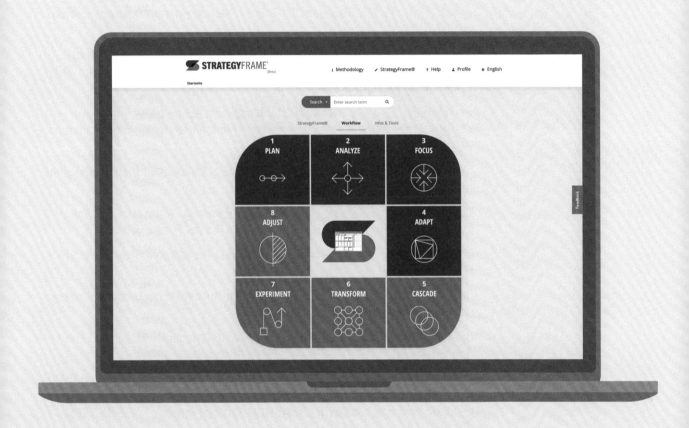

SOURCES

Adidas Group (3/10/2022): Press release: ADIDAS präsentiert Wachstums-strategie bis 2025: Own the game, https://www.adidas-group.com/de/ medien/ newsarchiv/pressemitteilungen/2021/adidas-prasentiert-wachstums- strategie-bis-2025-own-the-game/, downloaded on 9/15/2022.

Ansoff, H. I. (1965): Corporate Strategy, McGraw-Hill Inc., New York.

Ansoff, H. I. (1957): Strategies for Diversification, Harvard Business Review, Issue No. 10.

Anthony, S. D.; Gilbert, C. G.; Johnson, M. W. (2017): Dual Transformation: How to Reposition Today's Business While Creating the Future, Harvard Business Review Press, Boston.

Bertelsmann SE & Co. KGaA (2021): Morgen ist schon heute, corporate website, https://www.bertelsmann.de/unternehmen/strategie/, downloaded on 9/10/2022.

Chandler, A. D. (1962): Strategy and Structure. Chapters in the History of the Industrial Enterprise, MIT Press, Boston.

Christensen, C. M. (2013): The Innovator's Dilemma. When New Technologies Cause Great Firms to Fail, Harvard Business Review Press, Boston.

Clear, J. (2018): Atomic Habits. Tiny Changes, Remarkable Results, Random House, New York.

Collins, J.; Porras, J. I. (2004): Built to Last: Successful Habits of Visionary Companies, Harper Business, New York.

Collins, J.C. (2001): Good to Great: Why Some Companies Make the Leap... And Others Don't, Harper Business, New York.

Collis, D. J. (2021): Why Do So Many Strategies Fail? Leaders focus on the parts rather than the whole, Harvard Business Review July-August, https:// hbsp. harvard.edu/product/R2104E-HCB-ENG, downloaded on 9/15/2022.

Damm, C. (2/7/2018): Aldi expandiert auf einem Markt, an den sich Lidl bislang noch nicht herangewagt hat, Business Insider, https://www.business-insider.de/wirtschaft/aldi-expandiert-auf-einem-markt-an-den-sich-lidl-noch-nicht-heranwagt-2018-2/, downloaded on 9/12/2022.

Data Bridge (04/2021): Global Canned Wine Market – Industry Trends and Forecast to 2028, https://www.databridgemarketresearch.com/reports/global-canned-wine-market, downloaded on 9/14/2022.

Darwin, C. (2018): The Origin of Species, Signet Press, Reprint, 2003.

Doerr, J. (2018): Measure What Matters: OKRs: The Simple Idea that Drives 10x Growth, Penguin Books, London.

Duggan, W. (2007): Strategic Intuition. The creative spark in human achievement, Columbia Business School Publishing, New York.

Duggan, W. (2013): Creative Strategy. A guide for innovation, Columbia Business School Publishing, New York.

Esch, F.-R. (2021): Purpose und Vision. Wie Unternehmen Zweck und Ziel erfolgreich umsetzen, Campus Verlag, Frankfurt am Main.

Ferstl, E. (2015): Punktgenau. Aphorismen. BoD.

Gelb, D. (11.06.2011): Jiro Dreams of Sushi. Magnolia Pictures.

Gottfredson, C; Mosher B. (2010): Innovative Performance Support: Strategies and Practices for Learning in the Workflow, McGraw-Hill, New York.

Hasso-Plattner-Institut Academy (2022): Was ist Design Thinking? https:// hpi- academy.de/design-thinking/was-ist-design-thinking/, downloaded on 9/17/2022.

Henderson, B. (1970): The Product Portfolio, The Boston Consulting Group, Boston.

Henderson, B. D. (1989): Origin of Strategy: What Business Owes Darwin and Other Reflections on Competitive Dynamics, Harvard Business Review, November-December.

Jonas, H. (6/11/1992): On receiving his honorary doctorate from Freie Universität Berlin, Fatalismus wäre Todsünde - Gespräche über Ethik und Mitverantwortung im dritten Jahrtausend, Hg. v. Dietrich Böhler im Auftrag des Hans Jonas-Zentrums e. V., Lit Verlag, Münster 2005.

Jung, H.; von Matt, J. R. (2011): Momentum. Die Kraft, die Werbung heute braucht, Lardon Media, Berlin.

Kahnemann D. (2011): Thinking Fast, Thinking Slow. Penguin Books, New York.

Kahnemann D.; Sibony O.; Sunstein C. R. (2021): Noise: A Flaw in Human Judgment. Harper Collins, London.

Kay, J.; King, M. (2020): Radical Uncertainty: Decision-Making Beyond the Numbers, WW Norton & Co, New York.

Keynes, J.M. (1924): The Treatise on Monetary Reform, Macmillan, London.

Kim, W. C.; Mauborgne, R. A. (2015): Blue Ocean Strategy. How to Create Uncontested Market Space and Make the Competition Irrelevant, Expanded Edition, Harvard Business Review Press, Boston.

Knacke, C. (2022): Trend und Innovationsmanagement, Wie Sie systematisches Trendmanagement einführen & Ihre Innovationsprozesse professionalisieren, Trendone Whitepaper https://www.trendone. com/whitepaper-trend-management-und-innovationsmanagement, downloaded on 9/10/2022.

Kotler, P., Armstrong, G. (2012): Principles of Marketing, Pearson Prentice Hall, Hoboken, New Jersey.

Kotter, J. P. (2011): Leading Change, Harvard Business Review Press, Boston.

Kotter, J. P. (2014): Accelerate: Building Strategic Agility for a Faster-Moving World, Harvard Business Review Press, Boston.

Kübler-Ross, E. (1969): On Death and Dying, Macmillan, New York.

Lafley, A. G.; Martini, R. L. (2013): Playing to Win: How Strategy Really Works, Harvard Business Review Press, Boston.

Markides, C. C. (2022): Don't Confuse Strategy with Lofty Goals, Harvard Business Review, https:// hbr.org/2022/06/dont-confuse-strategy-with-lofty-goals, downloaded on 9/10/2022.

McCall, M.; Lombardo, M. M.; Eichinger, R. A. (1996): Career Architect Development Planner, Lominger Limited, Minneapolis.

Menz, M; Kunisch, S; Birkinshaw, J; Collis, D. J.; Foss, N. J.; Hoskisson, R. E.; Prescott, J. E. (2021): Corporate Strategy and the Theory of the Firm in the Digital Age, Journal of Management Studies 58.

Mintzberg et al. (1995): The Strategy Process. Concepts, Contexts, Cases, Prentice Hall, Englewood Cliffs, N.J.

Mintzberg, H. (1994): The Rise and Fall of Strategic Planning, Prentice Hall, Englewood Cliffs, N.J.

Momentive (2022): Cascade Strategy Report 2022, https://www.cascade.app/ strategy-report-2022, downloaded on 9/10/2022.

Osterwalder, A. (2010): Business Model Generation. A Handbook for Visionaries, Game Changers, and Challengers, Wiley, New Jersey.

Oberholzer-Gee, F. (2021): Eliminate Strategic Overload, Harvard Business Review, May-June.

Pietersen W. (2001): Strategic Learning: How to Be Smarter Than Your Competition and Turn Key Insights into Competitive Advantage, Wiley, Hoboken, New Jersey.

Porter, M. E. (1980): Competitive Strategy: Techniques for Analyzing Industries and Competitors, Free Press, New York.

Porter, M. E. (1996): What is Strategy?, Harvard Business Review, November-December.

Quadbeck-Seeger, H. (2006): Im Labyrinth der Gedanken. Aphorismen und Definitionen, BoD.

Rumelt, R. (2022): The Crux: How Leaders Become Strategists, Profile Books, London.

Samuelson, P. (1938): A Note on the Pure Theory of Consumers' Behaviour, Economica 5.

Schoemaker, P. J. H. (1995): Scenario Planning: A Tool for Strategic Thinking, MIT Sloan Management Review 36.

Schumpeter, J. A. (1911): Theorie der wirtschaftlichen Entwicklung, Duncker & Humblot, Berlin.

Schumpeter, J. A. (1942): Capitalism, Socialism, Democracy, Harper & Brothers, New York.

Simon, H. (1998): Wettbewerb ist ein Verfahren, Faulenzer und Fleißige zu trennen, in Süddeutsche Zeitung 16.11.1998

Simon, H. (2007): Hidden Champions des 21. Jahrhunderts: Die Erfolgsstrategien unbekannter Weltmarktführer, Campus Verlag, Frankfurt am Main.

Sinek, S. (2011): Start with Why. How Great Leaders Inspire Everyone to Take Action, Penguin Books, London.

Statista (2022): Bevölkerung - Zahl der Einwohner in Deutschland nach relevanten Altersgruppen am 31. Dezember 2021. https://de.statista.com/ statistik/ daten/studie/1365/umfrage/bevoelkerung-deutschlands-nach-altersgruppen/, downloaded on 9/15/2022.

Strategy& (17.01.2019): Drei Viertel der Manager zweifeln den Erfolg der Strategie des eigenen Unternehmens an, Press release from January 17, 2019, https://www.strategyand.pwc.com/de/ de/presse/2019/zweifel-an-erfolgsstrategie.html, downloaded on 9/10/2022.

Sull, D.; Homkes, R.; Sull, C. (2015): Why Strategy Execution Unravels – and What to Do About It, Harvard Business Review, March.

Taleb, N. N. (2012): Antifragile. Things that Gain from Disorder, Penguin Books, New York.

Wittgenstein, L. (1918): Tractatus logico-philosophicus, Routledge, Milton Park.

THANKS FROM BOTH OF US

Corporate strategies are seldom conceived and brought to life by individuals acting alone. If strategists take time out to think, they need other people to look after the day-to-day routine and keep the business running. That's why we are firmly convinced that strategy making is teamwork. And teamwork always works when we follow a shared target vision.

Writing a book is teamwork too – but not so much, because this book has two authors with a shared target vision. Instead, we would not have been capable of putting our thoughts, experiences, and insights to digital paper if we hadn't had many supporters who shared our target vision, took over our tiresome daily routines and necessities patiently and indulgently during the writing phase and inspired, motivated and corrected us sympathetically.

TO OUR TEAM, WITHOUT ANY CHRONOLOGY OR PRIORITY,
BUT WITH HEARTFELT THANKS AND HUMILITY:

WILLIE PIETERSEN, Retired C-Suite executive, Professor of Practical Management at Columbia Business School, inventor of the Strategic Learning Cycle and a source of inspiration to us to think strategy as a learning task and in its practical application for people. Thx Willie, never retire!
www.williepietersen.com

EVA ZIMMERMANN, designer, for the amazing and unique clarity in her visualization of our ideas and also of the entire book. Thanks for these unique creations – and of course for keeping your nerve in countless cycles of coordination and corrections.
www.zmn.design

OLIVER KERN, our "partner in crime" for the StrategyFrame® as an SaaS offering and connector of the worlds of strategy and learning on all aspects of the topic of "workflow learning" and electronic performance support systems.

OUR CUSTOMERS from more than 100 strategy and transformation processes for their confidence to tread new paths "with us".

AND LASTLY OUR FAMILIES: Amber, Brit, and Zoe, as well as Nicole, Sebastian, and Sammy, without whose backing, understanding for long nights, lonely weekends and holidays as well as uplifting words this book would never have been published.

ABOUT US

CHRISTIAN UNDERWOOD

Christian is an entrepreneur and consultant with more than 15 years' consultancy experience in strategy, transformation and innovation processes in SMEs, family-owned and listed companies. He is also a co-founder and CEO of SaaS provider StrategyFrame® GmbH as well as co-host of the leading German strategy podcast "Hoffnung ist keine Strategie" [Hope is not a strategy]. He has a Magister (graduate degree) from the University of Heidelberg in Political Science South Asia, an MBA in General Management from WHU and a Postgraduate Diploma in Digital Business from EMERITUS (MIT Sloan + Columbia Business School).
underwood.de

PROF. DR. JÜRGEN WEIGAND

Jürgen has served as Deputy Dean and Associate Dean for Academic Programs at WHU – Otto Beisheim School of Management since 2015. He is Chair Professor of Economics at the Institute for Industrial Organization and Academic Director of the Center for Responsible Leadership at WHU. His specialist areas include corporate and competitive strategy, antitrust and corporate governance. He has more than 20 years' experience in consultancy with companies and in the public sector. He is also a co-founder and Chairman of the Advisory Board of StrategyFrame® GmbH as well as co-host of the podcast "Hoffnung ist keine Strategie" [Hope is not a strategy].
juergenweigand.com

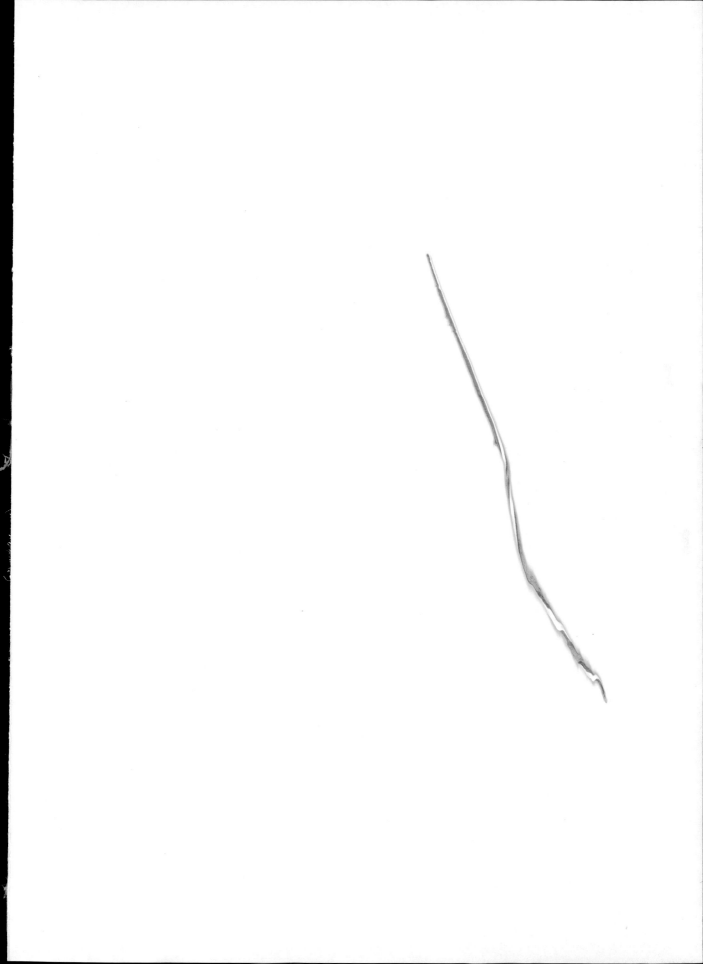